The Jolly Herring

77 songs - folk and pop

chosen by Roger Bush
with drawings by Roy Bentley

A & C Black Ltd · London

First published 1980 by A. & C. Black (Publishers) Ltd. 35 Bedford Row London WC1R 4JH
ISBN 0 7136 2095 1 non-net (spiral, limp) 0 7136 2094 3 net (spiral, laminated card)
A WORDS ONLY edition (ISBN 0 7136 2096 X) is also available
Printed in Great Britain by Hollen Street Press Limited, Slough, Berkshire

Contents

. . . but the atmosphere's good and there's no shortage of great old stories.

28 MacPherson's farewell
29 Hangman
30 Whiskey in the jar
31 Turpin hero
32 High Germany
33 The bonnie lass o' Fyvie
34 John Barleycorn
35 Casey Jones
36 The Gypsy Davey
37 The gypsy rover
38 The Ellen Vannin tragedy

The country folk sit in one corner . . .

39 Dorset is beautiful
40 Fling it here, fling it there
41 Green lanes
42 Land of the old and grey
43 If it wasn't for the 'ouses in between

. . . and the matelots in another.

44 The drunken sailor
45 Can't you dance the polka
46 Haul away Joe
47 Santy Anna
48 The leaving of Liverpool
49 The Marco Polo
50 The wreck of the John B
51 Pay me my money down
52 Fulera mama
53 Whip jamboree

The old heartaches ache once more . . .

54 The Curragh of Kildare
55 The girl I left behind
56 Sweet Willie
57 Handsome Molly
58 The water is wide
59 Once I had a sweetheart
60 Liverpool Lou

. . . but our host, preferring a cheerful atmosphere, interrupts with "Have a round on me" . . .

61 The orchestra song
62 I'm not strong, Sir
63 Have you seen the ghost of Tom ?
64 Whose pigs are these ?
65 The barmaid from Swale

. . . and finally gets us together for some old favourites . . .

66 Lady Madonna
67 Penny Lane
68 The windmills of your mind
69 An Eriskay love lilt
70 Sailing
71 The yellow rose of Texas
72 Messing about on the river
73 The lightning tree
74 I can see for miles
75 Scarborough Fair
76 The wild mountain thyme

. . . to all of which we can only say . . .

77 Thank U very much

Accompaniments

Nearly all the songs are provided with a simple piano accompaniment, but a few, mostly authentic folksongs, are so unsuited to piano accompaniment that we have left them without. Guitar chords are provided, though guitarists are encouraged to regard them as suggestions rather than instructions; many of the songs can be harmonized in different ways. In some cases we've offered alternative chords, the second suggestion placed in brackets above the first.

Deciding how to accompany a song requires flexibility. Folksongs often sound well with guitar accompaniment, but there are other, more authentic, ways of performing them. They may be sung unaccompanied, or with melody instruments (e.g. violin, flute or recorder) playing the tune in unison with the voice. At the other end of the scale, many of the songs in this book can be played and sung by a fully-fledged pop group. The members of the group will have to work out how they go about this, and in particular the rhythm section will be responsible for keeping the performance buoyant and alive. Competent enough players will want to insert instrumental breaks, probably building on chord sequences from the songs; *I'm the urban spaceman* (22) and *I can see for miles* (74) both lend themselves to this approach, and many of the other songs could be done in the same way.

For a number of songs we've made particular accompanying or performing suggestions. Some ideas for simple two-part singing are introduced(songs 10, 18, 51, 52, 56), and songs 61-65 are rounds.

Song 23 (*Colonel Fazackerley*) has the composer's own piano arrangement.
Other piano arrangements are by:
- Beatrice Harrop (songs 6, 8, 9, 39, 45, 47, 48, 54, 72)
- Beatrice Harrop/Roger Bush (2)
- Beatrice Harrop/Peter Nickol (14)
- Sheena Hodge (3, 11, 12, 16, 17, 29, 31, 40, 44, 46, 49, 50, 60)
- Peter Nickol (1, 4, 5, 18-20, 22, 25, 27, 28, 30, 34, 37, 38, 41, 43, 51, 66-70, 74, 76)
- Peter Nickol/Roger Bush (26, 58, 75)
- Timothy Roberts (13, 15, 24, 35, 71, 73, 77)
- Timothy Roberts/Roger Bush (7)
- Timothy Roberts/Peter Nickol (21)

Descants and second melody parts (in songs 28, 37, 56, 75) are by Peter Nickol.
Guitar chords are by Roger Bush.

Guitar chords

These are all the guitar chords found in this book.

A cross above a string means that it should not be sounded. A bracket linking two or more strings indicates that they should be held down simultaneously by the first finger.

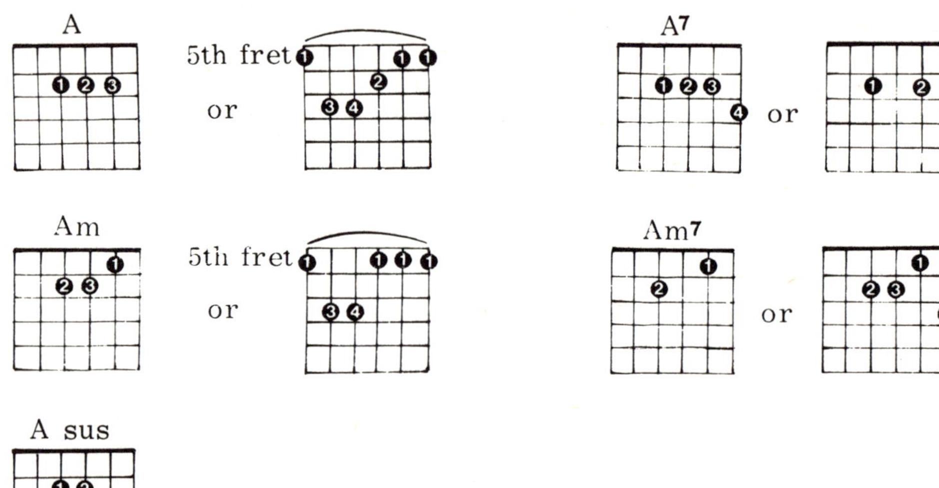

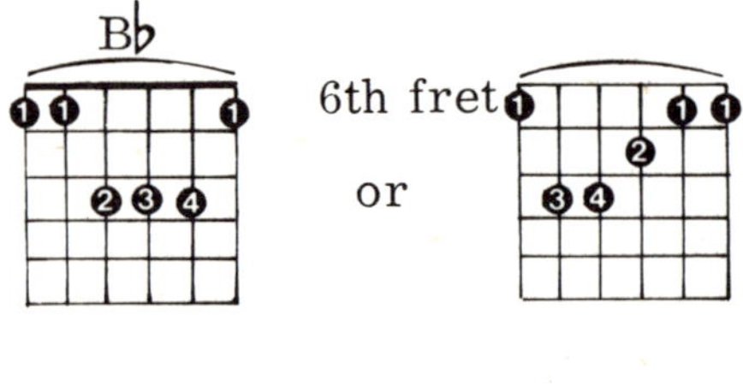

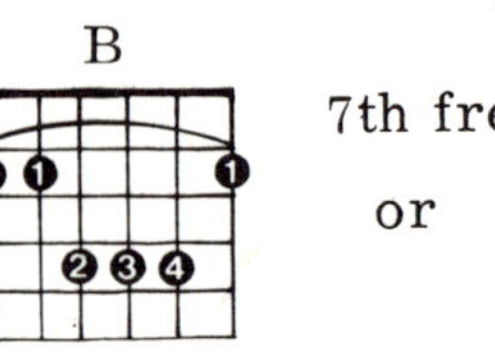

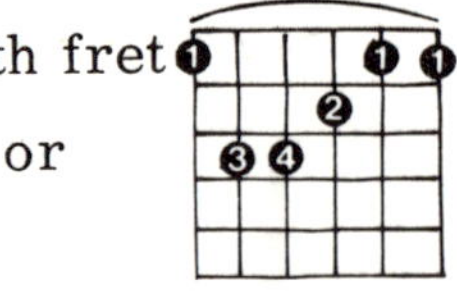

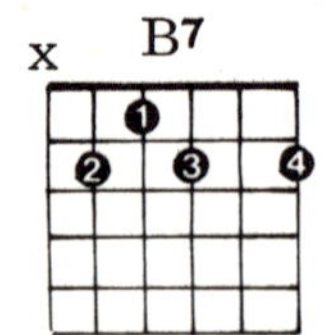

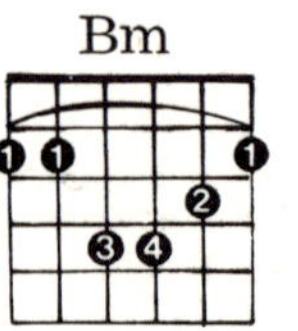

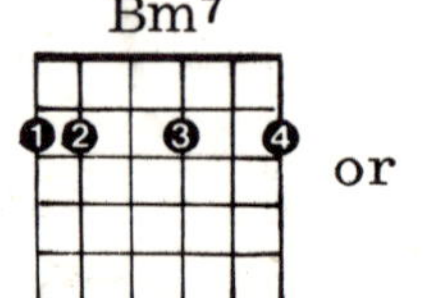

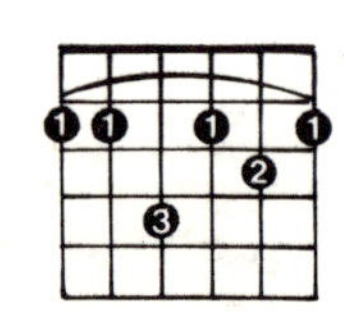

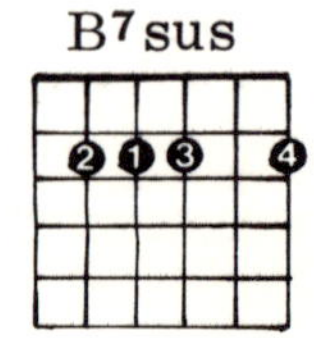

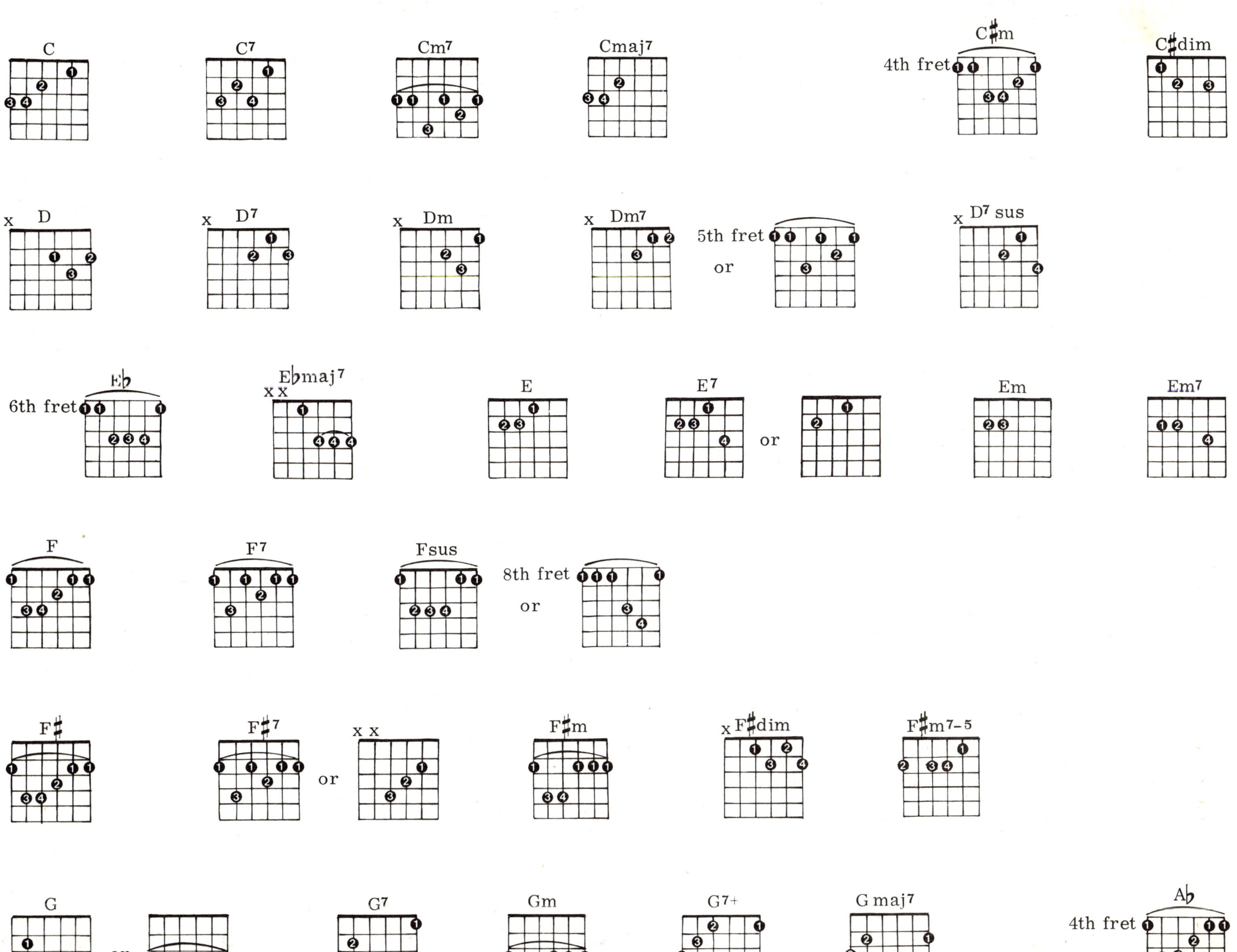
C
C7
Cm7
Cmaj7
C♯m
4th fret
C♯dim
D
D7
Dm
Dm7
5th fret
or
D7 sus
E♭
6th fret
E♭maj7
E
E7
or
Em
Em7
F
F7
Fsus
8th fret
or
F♯
F♯7
or
F♯m
F♯dim
F♯m7–5
G
or
G7
Gm
G7+
G maj7
A♭
4th fret

1 The Jolly Herring

1 Now what will I do with my herring's head?
Aye, what will I do with my herring's head?
I'll make it into loaves of bread.
Herring's head? Loaves of bread?
Aye, and all manner of things.

Of all the fish that live in the sea
The herring is the one for me.
Well, what do you say to such a thing?
Have I done well with my jolly herring?

2 Now what will I do with my herring's eyes?
Aye, what will I do with my herring's eyes?
I'll make them into puddings and pies.
Herring's eyes? Puddings and pies?
Herring's head? Loaves of bread?
Aye, and all manner of things.
Of all the fish that live in the sea . . .

3 Now what will I do with my herring's gills?
Aye, what will I do with my herring's gills?
I'll make them into window sills.
Herring's gills? Window sills?
Herring's eyes? Puddings and pies?
Herring's head? Loaves of bread?
Aye, and all manner of things.
Of all the fish that live in the sea . . .

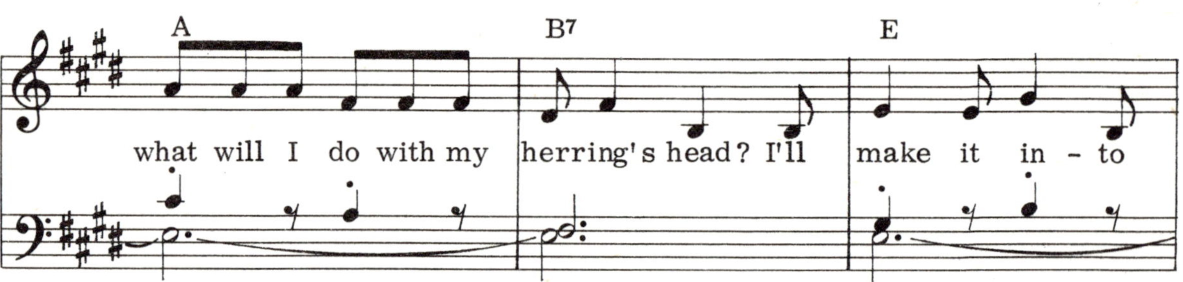

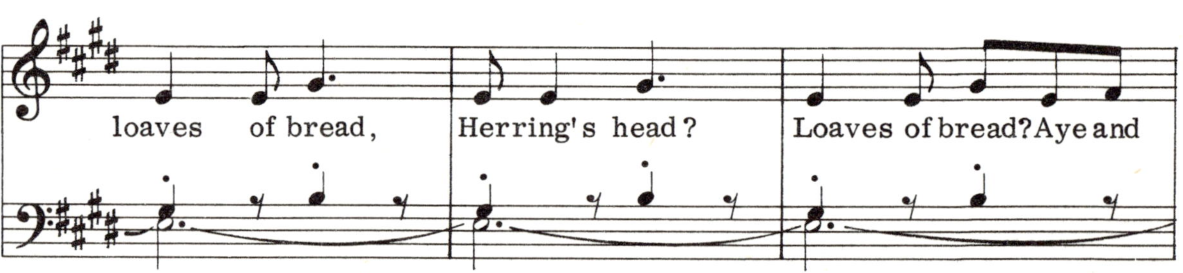

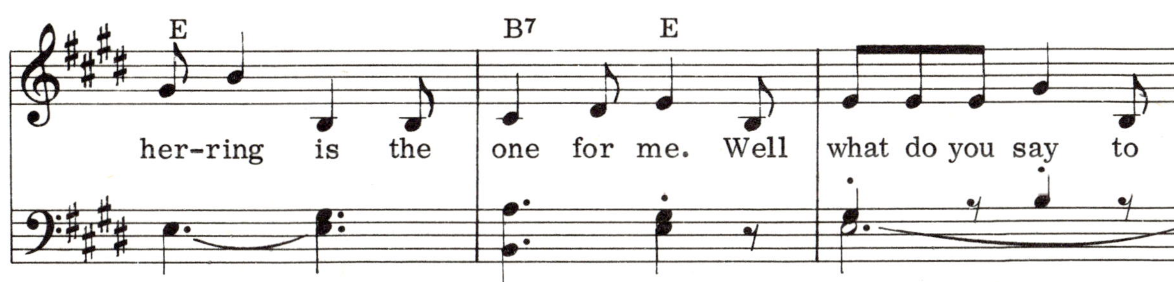

traditional

4 Now what will I do with my herring's back?
Aye, what will I do with my herring's back?
I'll make it into a fishing smack.
Herring's back? Fishing smack?
Herring's gills? Window sills?
Herring's eyes? Puddings and pies?
Herring's head? Loaves of bread?
Aye, and all manner of things.
Of all the fish that live in the sea . . .

5 Now what will I do with my herring's fins?
Aye, what will I do with my herring's fins?
I'll make them into needles and pins.
Herring's fins? Needles and pins?
Herring's back? Fishing smack?
Herring's gills? Window sills?
Herring's eyes? Puddings and pies?
Herring's head? Loaves of bread?
Aye, and all manner of things.
Of all the fish that live in the sea . . .

6 Now what will I do with my herring's tail?
Aye, what will I do with my herring's tail?
I'll make it into a barrel of ale.
Herring's tail? Barrel of ale?
Herring's fins? Needles and pins?
Herring's back? Fishing smack?
Herring's gills? Window sills?
Herring's eyes? Puddings and pies?
Herring's head? Loaves of bread?
Aye, and all manner of things.
Of all the fish that live in the sea . . .

2 The mountain dew

1 Let grasses grow and the waters flow
in a free and easy way,
But give me enough of the rare old stuff
that's made near Galway Bay.
And policemen all from Donegal,
Sligo and Leitrim too,
We'll give them the slip and we'll take a sip
of the real old mountain dew.

Hi the diddle-y-I-dillum
diddle-y doodle-I-dillum
Diddle-y doo-ri diddle-y-di day,
Hi the diddle-y-I-dillum
diddle-y doodle-I-dillum
Diddle-y doo-ri diddle-y-di day.

2 At the foot of the hill there's a neat little still
where the smoke curls up to the sky.
By the smoke and the smell you can plainly tell
that there's poteen, boys, nearby,
For it fills the air with a perfume rare,
and betwixt both me and you,
As home we roll we can drink a bowl
or a bucket of mountain dew.

3 Now learned men who use the pen
have wrote the praises high
Of the sweet poteen from Ireland green,
distilled from wheat and rye.
Away with pills, it will cure all ills,
for pagan, Christian or Jew,
So take off your coat and grease your throat
with the real old mountain dew.

traditional

3 The gulls o' Invergordon

1 In Invergordon by the sea
they've built a new distillery,
And all the gulls are on the spree
that live in Invergordon.
The mash that's flowing from the still
they gobble down wi' right good will
And every gull can hold his gill
that lives in Invergordon.

Dirumadoo-a-dirumaday
Dirumadoo-a-daddy-o,
Dirumadoo-a-dirumaday
The gulls o' Invergordon.

2 A Glesca gull came from the Clyde
in Invergordon to reside,
He got himself half stupefied
wi' the gulls o' Invergordon.
And then he found to his surprise
that he was hardly fit to rise
And flying kind of side-a-wise
when he left Invergordon.
Dirumadoo-a-dirumaday . . .

3 Now when we die some people say
we come back in some other shape.
Oh, how I'd like to come and stay
as a gull in Invergordon.
Dirumadoo-a-dirumaday,
reincarnation would be gay,
A kind o' perpetual Hogmanay
wi' the gulls o' Invergordon.
Dirumadoo-a-dirumaday . . .

Glesca: Glasgow

(or D - - - - E)
A E D A E A
ev - 'ry gull can hold his gill that lives in In - ver - gor - don.

Chorus
D E A G
Di - ru - ma - doo - a - di - ru - ma - day Di - ru - ma - doo - a - dad - dy - o.

A D E A E A
Di - ru - ma - doo - a - di - ru - ma - day, The gulls o' In - ver - gor - don.

4 Right said Fred

2 "Right" said Fred,
"Have to take the door off,
Need more space to shift the so-and-so."
Had bad twinges
Taking off the hinges,
And it got us nowhere,
And so we had a cuppa tea, and

"Right" said Fred,
"Have to take the wall down,
That there wall is gonna have to go."
Took the wall down,
Even with it all down
We was getting nowhere
And so we had a cuppa tea,

And Charlie had a think,
And he said "Look, Fred,
I got a sort of feeling,
If we remove the ceiling,
With a rope or two
We could drop the blighter through."

"All right" said Fred,
Climbing up a ladder,
With his crowbar gave a mighty blow.
Was he in trouble,
Half a ton of rubble
Landed on top of his dome.
Charlie and me had another cuppa tea,
And then we went home.

Spoken: I said to Charlie "We'll just have to leave it standing on the landing, that's all." Trouble with Fred is, he's too hasty. Never get nowhere if you're too hasty . . .

words: Myles Rudge
music: Ted Dicks

5 Hole in the ground

1 There I was digging this hole,
Hole in the ground, so big and sorta round it was,
And there was I digging it deep,
It was flat at the bottom and the sides were steep,
When along comes this bloke in a bowler
Which he lifted and scratched his head,
Oh, he looked in the hole, poor demented soul,
And said:

"Don't dig it there, dig it elsewhere,
It shouldn't be round, it ought to be square.
The shape of it's wrong, it's much too long,
And you can't put a hole where a hole don't belong."

2 There was I stood in my hole,
Shovelling earth for all that I was worth I was,
And there was him standing up there,
So grand and official with his nose in the air,
So I gave him a look sort of sideways,
And I leaned on my shovel and sighed,
Oh, I lit me a fag, and having took a drag,
Replied:

"Just couldn't bear to dig it elsewhere,
I'm digging it round 'cos I don't want it square.
If you disagree, doesn't bother me,
'Cos this is the place where the hole's gonna be."

3 There we were discussing this hole,
Hole in the ground, so big and sorta round it was,
It's not there now, the ground's all flat,
And beneath it is the bloke in the bowler hat.
And that's that.

GUITAR CHORDS: There are various ways of playing the G7+ chord, but guitarists may prefer the effect of a simpler chord, such as G7.

C G7 C G7+ C A7 Dm7 G7
head, Oh, he looked in the hole, poor demented soul, and said:
C G7+ C G7+ C G7+ C C7
"Don't dig it there, dig it else-where, it shouldn't be round, it ought to be square, The
F E7 (E♭) D7 G7+ C G7+
shape of it's wrong, it's much too long, and you can't put a hole where a hole don't be-long."
C G7+ C G7+ C G7+ C E7 Am7 D7
3. There we were dis-cussing this hole, hole in the ground, so big and sorta round it was, it's
G7 B♭7 A7 Dm D7 G7 C G7+ F7 C
not there now, the ground's all flat, and be-neath it is the bloke in the bow-ler hat. And that's that.
words: Myles Rudge music: Ted Dicks

6 Drill, ye tarriers, drill

1 Every morning at seven o'clock
There are twenty tarriers drilling at the rock
And the boss comes round and says "Keep still,
And come down heavy on the cast-iron drill."

And drill, ye tarriers, drill,
Drill, ye tarriers, drill.
Well, you work all day for the sugar in your tay,
Down behind the railway,
And drill, ye tarriers, drill. And blast. And fire.

2 Now our new foreman was Gene McCann,
By golly he was a blinken man.
Last week a premature blast went off,
And a mile in the air went Big Jim Goff.
And drill, ye tarriers, drill . . .

3 Next time payday comes around
Jim Goff a dollar short was found,
When asked what for, got this reply:
"You were docked for the time you were up in the sky."
And drill, ye tarriers, drill . . .

4 Now the boss was a fine man down to the ground
And he married a lady six feet round,
She baked good bread, and she baked it well,
But she baked it hard as the holes in —
And drill, ye tarriers, drill . . .

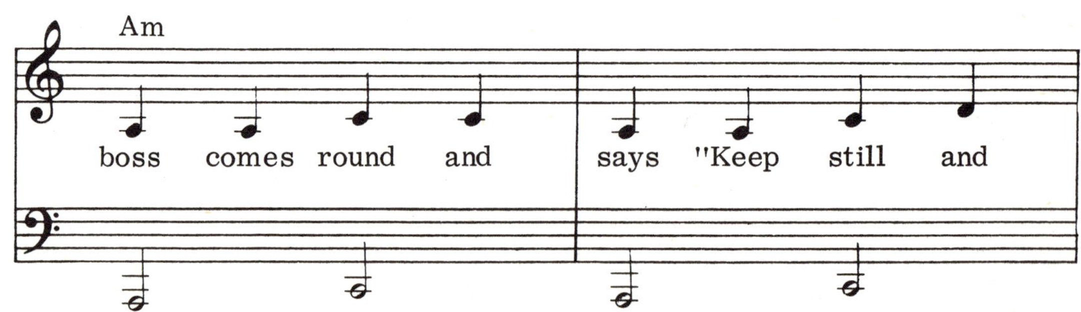

words and music: Thomas F. Casey

7 Indeed I would

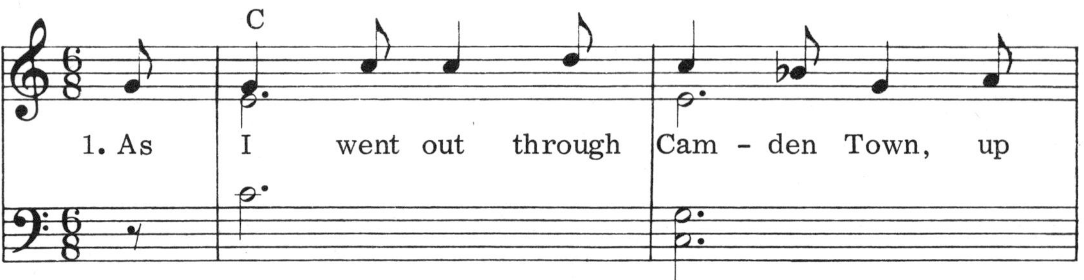

1 As I went through Camden Town, up came a Murphy truck,
And a gombeen man he said to me "Would you
like to shift some muck?"

O indeed I would
Don't you know I would,
With me right fol del the diddle-do,
Indeed I would.

2 He got me by the collar and he dropped me on the floor,
There was fifty Tipperary men and from Galway twenty more,
O indeed there was
Don't you know there was . . .

3 We raced along the road until the ganger gave a shout,
"Get down into the trench, me boys, and start to throw it out."
O indeed he did
Don't you know he did . . .

words: Ewan MacColl
music: Irish traditional

4 I grabbed me pick and shovel and I started for to dig,
And the fella right in front of me was grunting
like a pig,
O indeed he was
Don't you know he was . . .

5 Says I "If you keep on like that you'll be dying
for the job."
The ganger man he heard me and he shouted "Shut
your gob."
O indeed he did
Don't you know he did . . .

6 The ganger came from Skibbereen, he'd been a drover then,
Instead of driving cattle now he works at driving men,
O indeed he does
Don't you know he does . . .

7 Now here's a piece of good advice, it is the golden rule,
When they call you a good worker, it's a nickname
for a fool.
O indeed it is
Don't you know it is . . .

gombeen man: an extortionate middleman

8 Settle-Carlisle railway

1 In the year of '69 they planned to run a train
From Settle to Carlisle all across the mountain range.
They employed three thousand navvies to build this mighty road,
And across the fells to Appleby that old steam engine rolled.

And it's:
Up in the morning, lads, in wind, snow or hail,
Hold fast to your hammers, lads, and lay another rail.

2 It's 72 miles from Settle to Carlisle,
Across the roughest country in the British Isles.
They said it would take four years but it took them nearer seven,
And the first twenty miles sent four hundred men to heaven.
And it's . . .

3 And when the winter came it froze them to the floor,
It blew them off the viaducts and it killed them on Blea Moor.
Some died of the smallpox and some of cholera;
Chapal and St Leonards have many buried there.
And it's . . .

4 So if you ride this famous line across the heathered fells,
When crossing Ribblehead Viaduct remember the tale I tell.
There's Mallerstang and Aisgill and the Dent Dale's lovely wilds,
And navvy-lads a-slaving from Settle to Carlisle.
And it's . . .

words and music: Mike Donald

9 Coal-hole cavalry

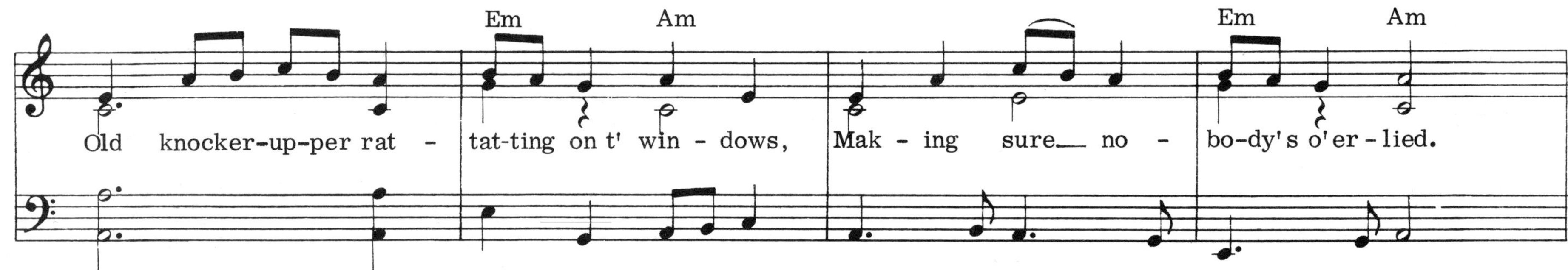

1 Early morning, dreaming is shattered,
One clitter-clatter on t' flags outside,
Old knocker-upper rat-tatting on t' window,
Making sure nobody's o'er-lied.

Clittering, clattering, coal-hole cavalry,
Galloping, rain or fine,
Clittering, clattering, coal-hole cavalry,
Galloping down to t' mine.

2 Father yawning, drizzle on t' window,
More clitter-clattering coming down th'hill,
Stairs are creaking, oven door banging,
Father waiting for Uncle Bill.

3 Mam is filling 'is bottle wi' water,
Clatter-clitter-clatter and a rattle on t' latch.
Clogs in t' lobby and talking quiet,
Arguing t' toss about Sunday's match.

4 Come on, Billy lad, best get going,
Clatter-clitter-clatter an' t' front door bang,
Going down to t' mucky old coal-pit,
Hear t' pit-hat and snap-tin clang.

5 Colliers riding a million horses,
Clatter-clitter-clatter all over t' world.
Look out, Injuns! Cavalry's coming,
Picks and shovels and banners unfurled.

6 Buzzer's blowing a sound of victory,
Clatter-clitter-clattering's over and done.
All t' world's quiet and sleep is coming,
Wish I were a collier, it must be fun.

snap-tin: a tin for holding sandwiches, hung on the belt.

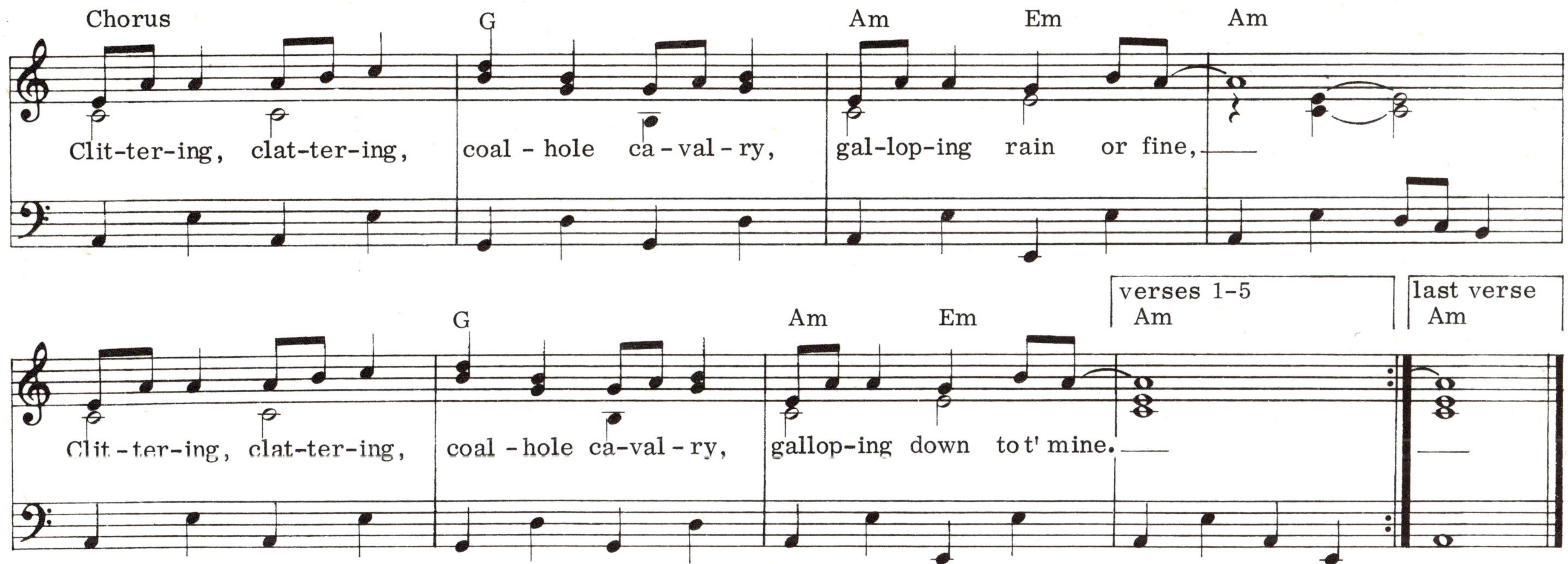

words and music: Ted Edwards

Ted Edwards, who wrote this song, says, "I was brought up in Wigan when it was a coal-mining community, and all the men, including eventually myself, were colliers. At about 5 a.m. every morning, when I was a very small child, I would be awakened by the clitter-clatter of a pair of clogs on the pavement (flags). Then there would be a tapping on the window. This was the old knocker-up, who had a long pole with a bit of wire on the end, waking all the miners up for work. Soon there would be about fifty pairs of clogs galloping down the road, sounding like a cavalry charge, and I used to imagine that this was the Coal-hole Cavalry charging down to the mine to kick out the Indians who'd taken over the coal mine during the night."

10 This old hammer

1 This old hammer killed John Henry
This old hammer killed John Henry
This old hammer killed John Henry
But it won't kill me, won't kill me.

2 This old hammer shines like silver
This old hammer shines like silver
This old hammer shines like silver
But it rings like gold, rings like gold.

3 This old hammer killed John Henry
This old hammer killed John Henry
This old hammer killed John Henry
But it won't kill me, won't kill me.

traditional

This song can be sung by two voice-parts in canon, the second part entering half a bar after the first:

first voice: This old hammer——killed John Henry——This old hammer
second voice: This old hammer——killed John Henry—— *etc.*

11 The broadside man

Same tune for verse and chorus

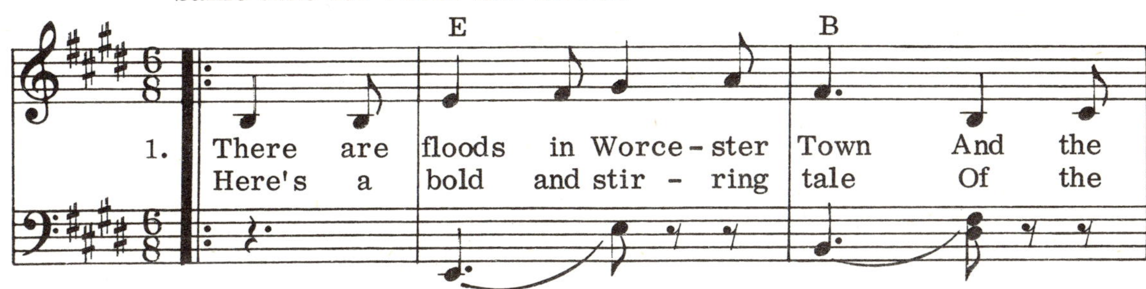

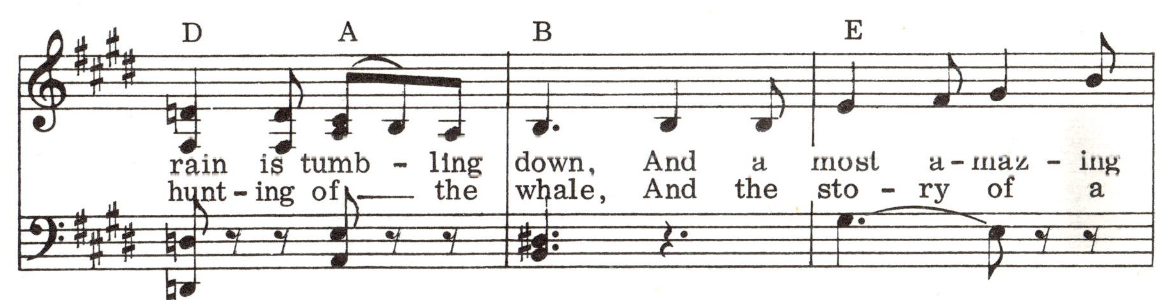

words and music: John Conolly and Bill Meek

1 There are floods in Worcester Town
And the rain is tumbling down
And a most amazing monster has been captured in the Dee.
Here's a bold and stirring tale
Of the hunting of the whale
And the story of a parson who was pressed away to sea.

Come and buy, come and buy,
Be you poor or genterye,
Gather round the broadside man and pay your money down.
Ballads long and short
And the best of every sort,
For a single paltry penny all the news of London Town.

2 Here's the finest sheets of all,
Fresh today from Stationers' Hall,
A newly-written ballad of Lord Nelson's victory.
Here's the news from all the courts,
Of the cases and reports,
And the rantings of a pirate who was hanged on Tyburn Tree.
Come and buy, come and buy . . .

3 Here's the story of a maid
Of the brisk and rambling trade,
Deceiving of a tinker who was taken by her charms,
And the story of a wife,
It's the truth upon my life,
Who came upon her husband rolling in the milkmaid's arms.
Come and buy, come and buy . . .

12 Timothy Winters

1 Timothy Winters comes to school
With eyes as wide as a football pool,
Ears like bombs and teeth like splinters:
A blitz of a boy is Timothy Winters.

2 His belly is white, his neck is dark,
And his hair is an exclamation mark.
His clothes are enough to scare a crow
And through his britches the blue winds
blow.

3 When teacher talks he won't hear a word
And he shoots down dead the arithmetic-bird,
He licks the patterns off his plate
And he's not even heard of the Welfare State.

4 Timothy Winters has bloody feet
And he lives in a house on Suez Street,
He sleeps in a sack on the kitchen floor
And they say there aren't boys like him any more.

5 Old Man Winters likes his beer
And his missus ran off with a bombardier,
Grandma sits in the grate with a gin
And Timothy's dosed with an aspirin.

6 The Welfare Worker lies awake
But the law's as tricky as a ten-foot snake,
So Timothy Winters drinks his cup
And slowly goes on growing up.

words: Charles Causley
music: Leon Rosselson

7 At Morning Prayers the Master helves
For children less fortunate than ourselves,
And the loudest response in the room is when
Timothy Winters roars "Amen!"

8 So come one angel, come on ten:
Timothy Winters says "Amen
Amen amen amen amen."
Timothy Winters, Lord.

Amen.

helves: a dialect word from north Cornwall used to describe the alarmed lowing of cattle (as when a cow is separated from her calf); a desperate, pleading note.

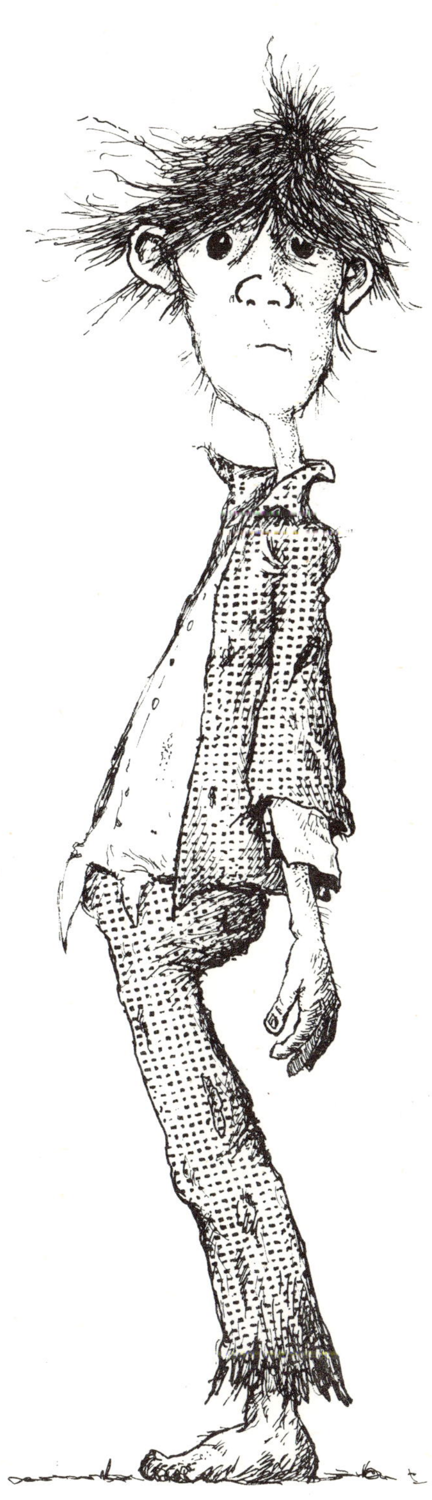

13 Pete was a lonely mongrel dog who lived in central Wigan, Lancs

1 Pete was a lonely mongrel dog
who lived in central Wigan.
He had a great thought one winter's day
while out for bones a-digging:
He'd change his life and he'd change his ways
and a sailor-man he'd be,
So he packed his tail and buried his bones
and off to sea went he.

Off to sea went, off to sea went,
off to sea went he-e-e,
Off to sea went, off to sea went,
off to sea went he.

2 He joined an English man-o'-war
as first mate to the captain,
They travelled far to many lands
where the trees were tall and champion.
He roamed the seas until he found
it wasn't what he'd dreamed:
There was no place to bury his bones
and his tail was a permanent green.
He'd change his life and he'd change his ways
and a soldier he would be,
So he buried his bones in the ocean deep
and off to war went he.

Off to war went, off to war went,
off to war went he-e-e,
Off to war went, off to war went,
off to war went he.

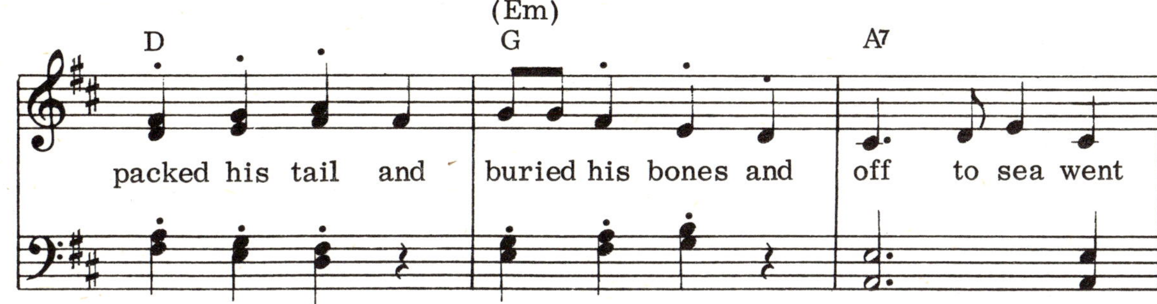

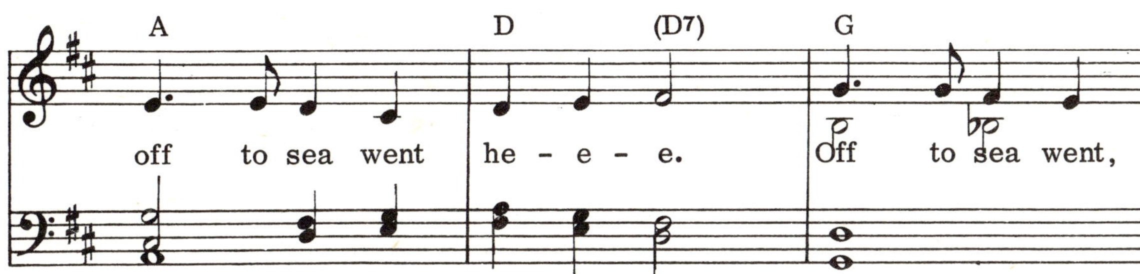

continued over . . .

3 He joined the Royal Artillery
as mascot to the battery.
Well he combed his hair and polished his tail
and did things very exactly.
Well they marched him up and down the square
and stood him to attention,
But when he'd chased the cook-house cat
they put him in detention.
He'd change his life and he'd change his ways
and an airman he would be,
So he swapped his guns for a set of wings
and off to fly went he.

Off to fly went, off to fly went,
off to fly went he-e-e,
Off to fly went, off to fly went,
off to fly went he.

4 He joined the Royal flying lads
as assistant navigator;
At finding his way from here to there
there never was anyone greater.
He flew through the air at incredible speeds
and sometimes upside-down,
And after a while he thought it was
much safer on the ground.
He'd change his life and he'd change his ways
and go back to his digging,
So he packed his tail and left his bones
and sniffed his way to Wigan.
He'd change his life and he'd change his ways
and he'd go back to his digging,
And spend his days in simple ways:
with his tail 'neath the trees of Wigan.

Verses 2-4
D (Em) G A7 D
(2) joined an En-glish man - o' - war as first mate to the cap-tain, They travelled far to
(Em) G A7 D A D
ma - ny lands where the trees were tall and champion. He roamed the seas un - til he found it
E7 A7 D (Em) G A
was-n't what he'd dreamed: there was no place to bu-ry his bones and his tail was a per ma-nent
D (A7) G D (E7) Em A7
green. He'd change his life and he'd change his ways and a sol - dier he would be, So he

words and music: John Meeks and Colin Radcliffe

14 Bob the pedigree sheepdog

1 I've got a dog, his name is Bob,
And I know he's a pedigree sheepdog,
'Cos if walkers stray on the Pennine Way
He'll prove he's a Dales-bred sheepdog,
And he'll fill the pen with assorted men,
Something to sharpen his teeth on,
And his picnic taste for salmon paste
Proves he's a Dales-bred sheepdog.

2 Now at sheepdog trials they come for miles
Just to see a pedigree sheepdog,
And his country fans all clap their hands
'Cos they know he's a Dales-bred sheepdog.
Whilst others leap to round up sheep
He's a nowhere-to-be-seen dog;
Knocking down Newcastle Brown
Proves he's a pint-size sheepdog.

3 Now cars and bikes and folks on hikes
Are clogging all the Dales up,
And if it goes on there won't be none
For our littermen to clean up.
But Bob works hard in his own farmyard,
He doesn't need a reason;
A tourist a day keeps pollution away,
And it's always open season.

4 A dog-food man with a can in his hand
Full of marrowbone jelly and noodles,
Said he's had enough of dogs from Crufts
And temperamental poodles.
He could take us far, make Bob a star:
Gold-plated kennels and houses.
But Bob gave a grin as he opened the tin
And took the backside out of his trousers.

words and music: Mike Donald and Roger Chappell

5 Now a man came round from the Skipton
  Pound,
In his hand he carried a summons,
'Cos Bob put a paw outside the law,
By gum, he is a rum 'un!
They'd had complaints to use restraints
And swore out an injuncture:
Bob's offence was he'd no licence
To practise acupuncture.
  So if you see Bob, the outlaw dog,
  Better leave him well alone,
  'Cos he likes little girls with long
    blonde curls
  Much better than a bone.

15 Football crazy

1 I have a favourite brother
and his christian name is Paul,
He's lately joined a football club
for he's mad about football.
He's two black eyes already,
and teeth lost from his gob,
Since Paul became a member
of that terrible football club.

For he's football crazy, he's football
mad,
The football it has taken away
the little bit of sense he had.
And it would take a dozen servants
to wash his clothes and scrub,
Since Paul became a member
of that terrible football club.

2 In the middle of the field, one afternoon,
the captain says, "Now Paul,
Would you kindly take this place-kick
since you're mad about football?"
So he took forty paces backwards,
shot off from the mark,
The ball went sailing over the bar
and landed in New York.

3 His wife she says she'll leave him
if Paulie doesn't keep
Away from football kicking
at night-time in his sleep;
He calls out "Pass, McGinty"
and other things so droll,
Last night he kicked her out of bed
and swore it was a goal!

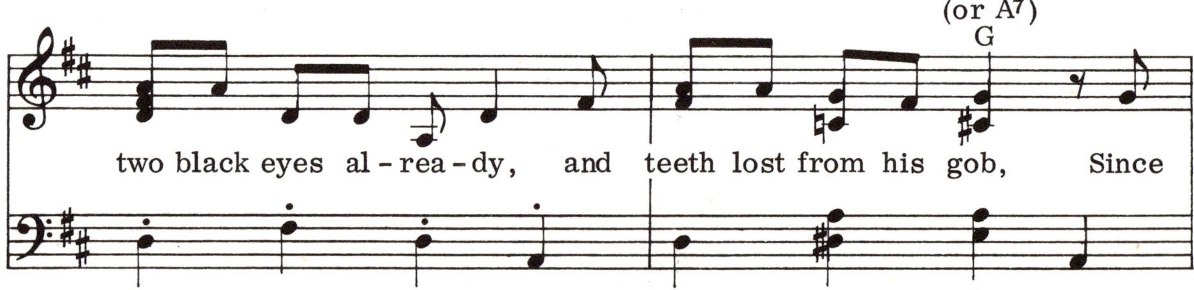

A7

foot - ball cra - zy, he's foot - ball mad. The

D A7 D

foot-ball it has ta-ken a-way the lit-tle bit of sense he had, And it would

(A7)
G

take a doz-en ser-vants to wash his clothes and scrub, since

D G D A7 D

Paul be-came a mem-ber of that ter-ri-ble foot-ball club.

traditional

16 Cotton Jenny

1 There's a house on a hill,
By a worn-down weathered old mill,
In the valley below where the river winds,
There's no such thing as bad times,
And a soft southern flame,
O, Cotton Jenny's her name,
She wakes me up when the sun goes down,
And the wheels of love go round,
Wheels of love go round, love go round,
Love go round, a joyful sound.
I ain't got a penny
For Cotton Jenny
To spend,
But then the wheels go round.

2 When the new day begins
I go down to the cotton gin,
And I make my time worth while to them,
Then I climb back up again.
And she waits by the door,
"O Cotton Jenny, I'm sore."
She rubs my feet while the sun goes down,
And the wheels of love go round,
Wheels of love go round, love go round . . .

3 In the hot sickly south,
When they say, "Well shut ma mouth,"
I can never be free from the cotton grind,
But I know what's mine.
A soft southern flame,
O, Cotton Jenny's her name,
She wakes me up when the sun goes down,
And the wheels of love go round,
Wheels of love go round, love go round . . .

words and music: Gordon Lightfoot

17 Leave them a flower

1 I speak on behalf of the next generation,
My sons and my daughters, their children to come.
What will you leave them for their recreation?
An oil slick, a pylon, an industrial slum?

Leave them a flower, some grass and a hedgerow,
A hill and a valley, a view to the sea.
These things are not yours to destroy as you want to,
A gift given once for eternity.

2 You plunder, you pillage, you tear and you tunnel,
Trees lying toppled, roots finger the sky.
Building a land for machines and computers.
In the name of progress the farms have to die.

3 Fish in an ocean polluted and poisoned,
The sand on the beaches is stinking and black.
You with your tankers, your banks and investments
Say "Never worry, the birds will come back."

4 When the last flower has dropped its last petal,
When the last concrete is finally laid,
The moon will shine cold on a nightmarish landscape,
Your gift to our children, the world which you've made.

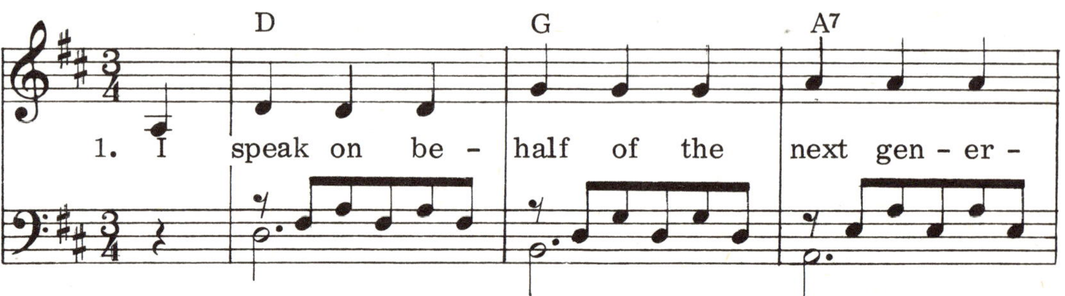

words and music: Wally Whyton

18 Across the hills

words and music: Leon Rosselson

1

voice A Across the hills black clouds are sweeping,
Carry poison far and wide,
And the grass has blackened underfoot,
And the rose has withered and died.

voice B But the rose is still as red, love,
and the grass is still as green,
And it must have been a shadow
in the distance you have seen,
Yes, it must have been a shadow you have seen.

2

voice A But can't you hear the children weeping?
Can't you hear the mournful sound?
And no birds sing in the twisted trees
In the silent streets around.

voicc B I can hear the children laughing
in the streets as they play,
And you must have caught the dying
of an echo far away,
Yes, it must have been an echo far away.

3

voice A But can't you see the white ash falling
From the hollow of the skies?
And the blood runs red down the blackened walls
Where a ruined city lies.

voice B I can see the red sun shining
in the park on the stream,
And you must have felt a shiver
from the darkness of a dream,
Yes, it must have been the darkness of a dream.

4

voice A And death shall reap a hellish harvest,
Make a desert of this land.

voice B But the rose is still as red, love,
and the grass is still as green,
And it must have been a shadow you have seen.
Yes, the rose is still as red, love,
and the grass is still as green,
And it must have been a shadow you have seen.

Leon Rosselson, who wrote this song, tells us, "The attitudes of the two voices are intended to be complementary rather than contradictory – I wasn't taking sides. Together, they seem to me to represent a more complete awareness – of the possibilities of life and the possibility of its destruction."

The last verse may be sung by the two voices together, like this:

19 Pollution

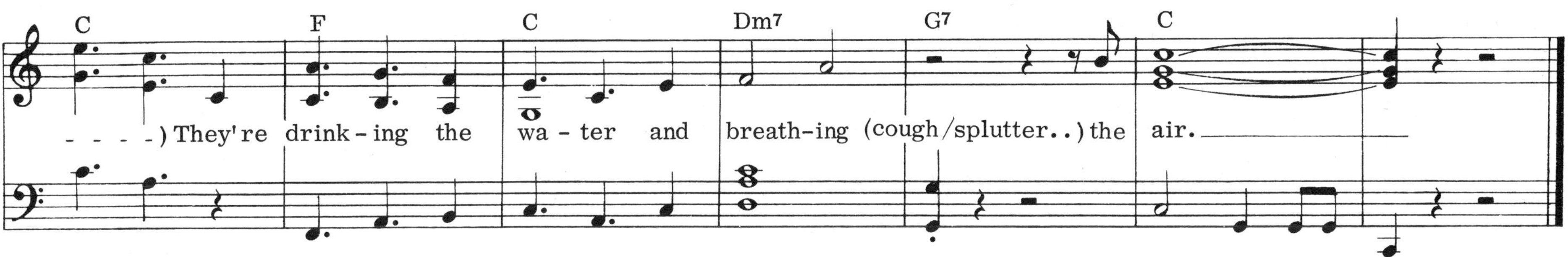

1 If you visit American city
You will find it very pretty.
Just two things of which you must beware:
Don't drink the water and don't breathe the air.

words and music: Tom Lehrer

Pollution, pollution, they got smog and sewage and mud,
Turn on your tap and get hot and cold running crud.

2 See the halibuts and the sturgeons
Being wiped out by detergeons.
Fish gotta swim and birds gotta fly,
But they don't last long if they try.

Pollution, pollution, you can use the latest toothpaste,
And then rinse your mouth with industrial waste.

3 Just go out for a breath of air,
And you'll be ready for Medicare.
The city streets are really quite a thrill,
If the hoods don't get you, the monoxide will.

Pollution, pollution, wear a gas-mask and a veil,
Then you can breathe, long as you don't inhale.

4 Lots of things there that you can drink,
But stay away from the kitchen sink,
Throw out your breakfast garbage and I've got a hunch
That the folks down-stream will drink it for lunch.

So go to the city, see the crazy people there,
Like lambs to the slaughter
They're drinking the water
And breathing (*cough . . . splutter*) the air.

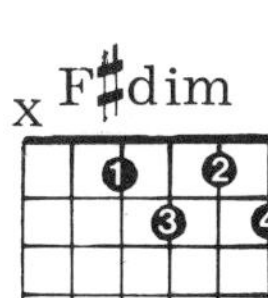

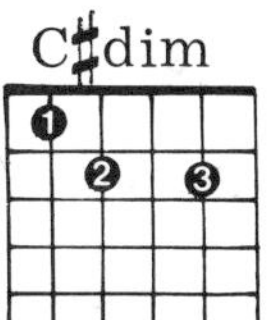

20 Air from "Hair"

Welcome, sulphur dioxide,
Hello, carbon monoxide,
The air, the air is everywhere.
Breathe deep while you sleep, breathe deep.

Bless you, alcohol blood stream,
Save me, nicotine lung steam,
Incense, incense is in the air.
Breathe deep while you sleep, breathe deep.

Cataclysmic ectoplasm,
Fall-out atomic orgasm,
Vapour and fume, at the stone of my tomb.
Breathing like a sullen perfume,
Eating at the stone of my tomb.

Welcome, sulphur dioxide,
Hello, carbon monoxide,
The air, the air is everywhere.
Breathe deep while you sleep, breathe deep (*cough*)
deep (*cough*) deep de deep (*cough*).

words: James Rado and Gerome Ragni
music: Galt MacDermot

21 My last cigarette

1 Tobacco, tobacco, I hate you I do,
Like Tarzan I'd look if it wasn't for you.
  But I'll give up the habit, I will even yet,
  When I've had just one more cigarette.
It wasn't the whisky, it wasn't the wine
That made such a wreck of this body of mine,
  But I'll give up the habit, I will even yet,
  When I've had just one more cigarette.

2 Under my eyes are a couple of bags,
I blame it all on to a packet of fags,
  But I'll give up the habit, I will even yet,
  When I've had just one more cigarette.
My teeth are all yellow and so is my tongue,
I breathe through a kipper, I call it a lung,
  But I'll give up the habit, I will even yet,
  When I've had just one more cigarette.

3 Nail in my coffin so pale and so thin,
I am a fool to keep driving you in.
  You say that you'll kill, how much do you bet?
  When I've had just one more cigarette.
I'll fling the packet away, away,
Fifty times in a week I say,
  Fling the packet away, away,
  When I've had just one more cigarette.

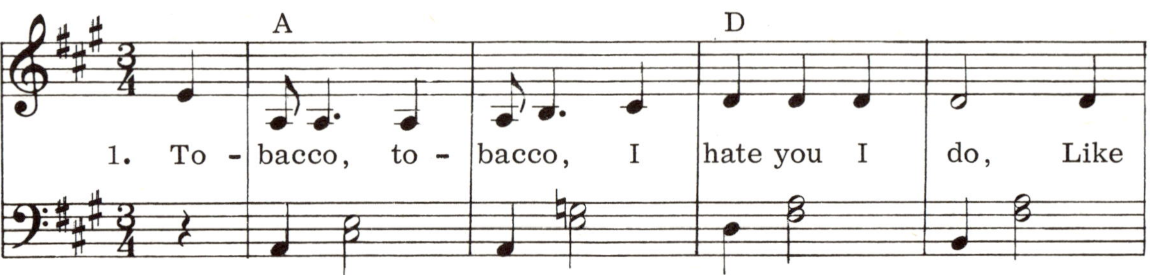

A E
was-n't the whis-ky, it was-n't the wine, that

D A
made such a wreck of this bo-dy of mine. But I'll

E
give up the hab-it, I will e-ven yet, when I've

A
had just one more ci-ga-rette.

words and music: Sydney Carter

22 I'm the urban spaceman

I'm the urban spaceman, baby, I've got speed,
I've got everything I need.
I'm the urban spaceman, baby, I can fly,
I'm a supersonic guy.
I don't feel pleasure, I don't feel pain,
If you were to knock me down I'd just get up again,
I'm the urban spaceman, I've got hairs on my chest,
I never get depressed.

I wake up every morning with a smile upon my face,
My natural exuberance spills out all over the place.
I'm the urban spaceman, baby, I'm making out,
I'm all about.

I'm the urban spaceman, I'm intelligent and keen,
Know what I mean?
I'm the urban spaceman, as a lover second to none,
It's a lot of fun.
I never let my friends down, I've never made a boob,
I'm a glossy magazine, an advert in the tube,
I'm the urban spaceman, baby, here comes the twist:
I don't exist.

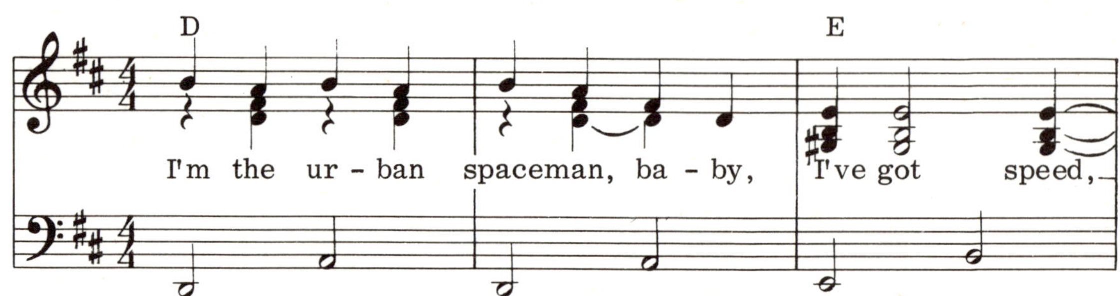

words and music: Neil Innes

23 Colonel Fazackerley

1 Colonel Fazackerley Butterworth-Toast
Bought an old castle complete with a ghost,
But someone or other forgot to declare
To Colonel Fazack that the spectre was there.

2 On the very first evening, while waiting to dine,
The Colonel was taking a fine sherry wine,
When the ghost, with a furious flash and a flare,
Shot out of the chimney and shivered, "Beware!"

3 Colonel Fazackerley put down his glass
And said, "My dear fellow, that's really first class!
I just can't conceive how you do it at all.
I imagine you're going to a Fancy Dress Ball?"

4 At this, the dread ghost gave a withering cry.
Said the Colonel (his monocle firm in his eye),
"Now just how you do it I wish I could think.
Do sit down and tell me, and please have a drink."

5 The ghost in his phosphorous cloak gave a roar
And floated about between ceiling and floor.
He walked through a wall and returned through a pane
And backed up the chimney and came down again.

6 Said the Colonel, "With laughter I'm feeling quite weak!"
(As trickles of merriment ran down his cheek).
"My house-warming party I hope you won't spurn.
You *must* say you'll come and you'll give us a turn!"

7 At this, the poor spectre—quite out of his wits—
Proceeded to shake himself almost to bits.
He rattled his chains and he clattered his bones
And he filled the whole castle with mumbles and moans.

8 But Colonel Fazackerley, just as before,
Was simply delighted and called out, "Encore!"
At which the ghost vanished, his efforts in vain,
And never was seen at the castle again.

9 "Oh dear, what a pity!" said Colonel Fazack.
"I don't know his name, so I can't call him back."
And then with a smile that was hard to define,
Colonel Fazackerley went in to dine.

words: Charles Causley
music: R. Vernon Beaumont

24 Where did you get that hat?

1 Now how I came to get this hat, 'tis very strange and funny,
Grandfather died and left to me his property and money;
And when the will it was read out, they told me straight and flat,
If I would have his money, I must always wear his hat!

Spoken: And everywhere I go, everyone shouts at me:

"Where did you get that hat?
Where did you get that tile?
Isn't it a nobby one, and just the proper style?
I should like to have one just the same as that!"
Where'er I go they shout "Hello! Where did you get that hat?"

2 If I go to the op'ra house, in the op'ra season,
There's someone sure to shout at me without the slightest reason.
If I go to a concert hall to have a jolly spree,
There's someone in the party who is sure to shout at me:

"Where did you get that hat? . . .

3 At twenty-one I thought I would to my sweetheart get married,
The people in the neighbourhood had said too long we'd tarried.
So off to church we went right quick, determined to get wed;
I had not long been in there when the parson to me said:

"Where did you get that hat? . . .

words and music: Charles Rolmas

4 I once tried hard to be MP but failed to get elected,
Upon a tub I stood, round which a thousand folks collected;
And I had dodged the eggs and bricks (which was no easy task),
When one man cried, "A question I the candidate would ask!"

Spoken: I told him that I was ready to reply to any question that could be put to me. The man said: "Thousands of British working people are anxiously awaiting enlightenment on the subject on which I am about to address you. It is a question of national importance, in fact: THE great problem of the day—and that is, Sir:

Where did you get that hat? . . .

5 When Colonel South, the millionaire, gave his last garden party,
I was among the guests who had a welcome true and hearty;
The Prince of Wales was also there, and my heart jumped with glee
When I was told the Prince would like to have a word with me.

Spoken: I was immediately presented to His Royal Highness who immediately exclaimed:

"Where did you get that hat? . . .

25 The Field of the Willows

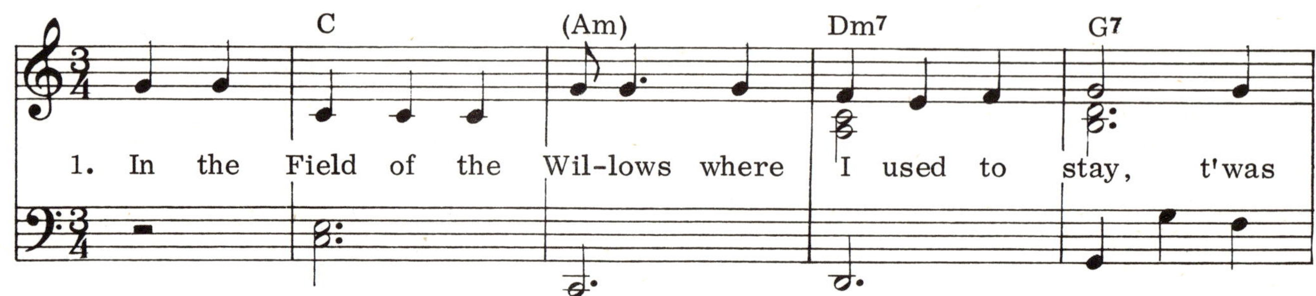

1 In the Field of the Willows where I used to stay
'Twas there that I washed all my troubles away
With the rain coming down every hour of the day
In the Field of the Willows so gay.

2 I saw an old man looking awfully queer
Sat under a tree with a bottle of beer
But when I got there he'd been dead for a year
In the Field of the Willows so gay.

3 To leave him unburied I knew was a sin
But I was too lazy a grave to begin
So I put on my boots and I trampled him in
In the Field of the Willows so gay.

4 As I took a walk by the river one day
Saw the minister's daughter a-heading my way.
She said "Come on, let's go and sit down in the hay,"
In the Field of the Willows so gay.

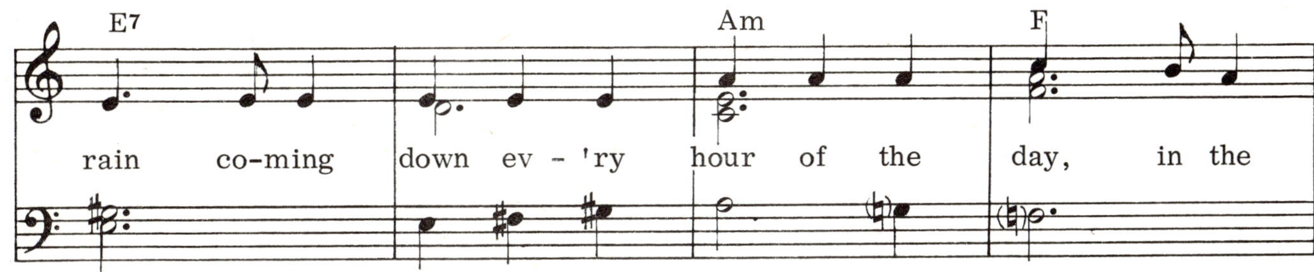

words and music: Dave Goulder

5 So into the dark of the barn we did creep
But it wasn't the maiden who sang me to sleep
But seventeen horses, twelve cows and a sheep
In the Field of the Willows so gay.

6 There's a hermit lives up on the mountain so high
And he washes himself every tenth of July.
The fish in the river roll over and die
In the Field of the Willows so gay.

7 A dashing young p'liceman went off on his trail
But he came back next morning all tattered and pale
With a pitchfork behind like a long wooden tail
In the Field of the Willows so gay.

8 In the Field of the Willows where I used to stay
'Twas there that I washed all my troubles away
With the rain coming down every hour of the day
In the Field of the Willows so gay.

26 Mole in a hole

1 Like the flowers, like the bees,
Like the woodlands and the trees,
I like the Byrds and their LPs
And I'm a refugee.

Wanna be a mole in a hole,
Making low and slow,
Wanna be a fly flying high
In the sky.
Wanna be a mole in a hole,
Making low and slow,
Wanna be a fly flying high
In the sky.

2 Well my feet are smelly and my hair's
a mess,
My teeth are yellow and I've got bad
breath,
I may look great but I feel like death
And I'm a refugee.
Wanna be a mole in a hole . . .

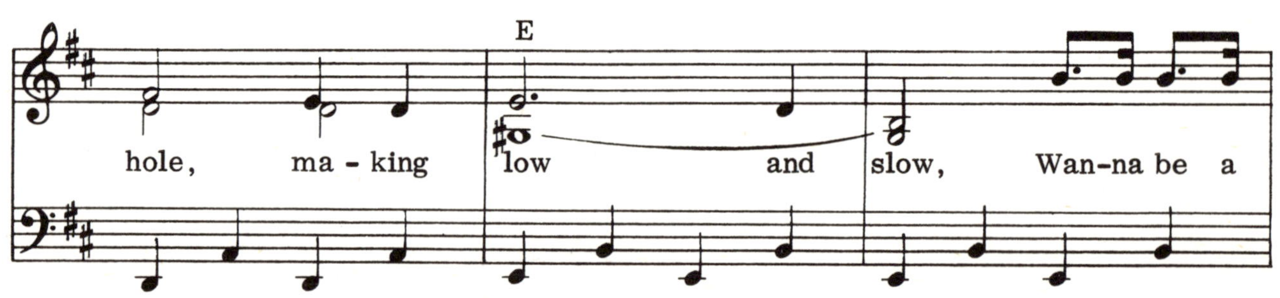

words and music: Mike Waterson

27 Hopalong Peter

1 Old Uncle Peter he got tight,
Started up to Heaven on a stormy night,
The road being rough and him not well,
He lost his way and went to ——

Hopalong Peter, where are you going?
Hopalong Peter, where are you going?
Hopalong Peter, won't you bear in mind
I ain't coming back till the gooseberry time.

2 Old Mother Hubbard and her dog were Dutch,
A bow-legged rooster and he hobbled on a crutch,
Hen chewed tobacco and the duck drank wine,
The goose played the fiddle on the pumpkin vine.
Hopalong Peter, where are you going? . . .

3 Down in the barnyard playing seven-up,
The old tom-cat and the little yellow pup,
The old Mother Hubbard, she's a-picking out the fleas,
The rooster in the cream jar up to his knees.
Hopalong Peter, where are you going? . . .

4 I've got a sweet gal in this here town,
If she weighs an ounce she weighs seven hundred pounds,
Every time my sweet gal turns once around,
The heel of her shoe makes a hole in the ground.
Hopalong Peter, where are you going? . . .

PIANO ACCOMPANIMENT
The piano part has the outline of the melody, but not all the repeated notes.

traditional

28 MacPherson's farewell

1 Farewell, ye dungeons dark and strong,
The wretch's destinie!
MacPherson's time will not be long,
On yonder gallows-tree.

Sae rantingly, sae wantonly,
Sae dauntingly gae'd he:
He play'd a spring, and danc'd it round
Below the gallows-tree.

2 O what is death but parting breath?
On many a bloody plain
I've dared his face, and in this place
I scorn him yet again!

3 Untie these bands from off my hands,
And bring to me my sword;
And there's no a man in all Scotland,
But I'll brave him at a word.

4 I've liv'd a life of sturt and strife;
I die by treacherie:
It burns my heart I must depart
And not avenged be.

5 Now farewell, light, thou sunshine bright,
And all beneath the sky!
May coward shame distain his name,
The wretch that dares not die!

sae: so
rantingly, wantonly: exultantly, wildly
dauntingly: courageously
gae'd: went
sturt: trouble

words: Robert Burns
music: traditional

James MacPherson was a famous and daring robber, who was finally caught in November 1700, tried before the sheriff of Banffshire, and hanged. According to tradition he was a tall, powerful man, the son of a Highlands lord and a gypsy mother. He spent his last hours writing a song, which he played on his violin while walking to the gallows. There, he offered the violin to whoever wished to have it, but no-one would take it and in indignation he broke it over his knee and scattered the pieces.

A broadsheet ballad telling the story appeared soon afterwards, and this was later re-modelled by the Scots poet Robert Burns into the defiant text given here. The sword, asked for in verse 3, actually survives: a huge weapon, six feet long.

PERFORMANCE

An accompanying melody is given here, labelled for recorders or violins but intended for any available instrument: flute, organ, electric guitar . . . (Of course not all instruments will find the part equally easy.) There's no reason why it should be played with every verse; it can be used with selected verses or, better still, as an instrumental break between verses.

29 Hangman

1 Slack your rope, hangman, slack it for a while,
I think I see my father coming riding many a mile.
Father, have you brought me hope or have you paid my fee,
Or have you come to see me hanging from the gallows tree?

I have not brought you hope,
I have not paid your fee.
Yes, I have come to see you hanging from the gallows tree.

2 (as verse 1, substituting "mother" for "father")
I have not brought you hope . . .

3 (as verse 1: "brother")
I have not brought you hope . . .

4 (as verse 1: "sister")
I have not brought you hope . . .

5 Slack your rope, hangman, slack it for a while,
I think I see my true love coming riding many a mile.
True love, have you brought me hope or have you paid my fee,
Or have you come to see me hanging from the gallows tree?

Yes, I have brought you hope,
Yes, I have paid your fee.
I have not come to see you hanging from the gallows tree.

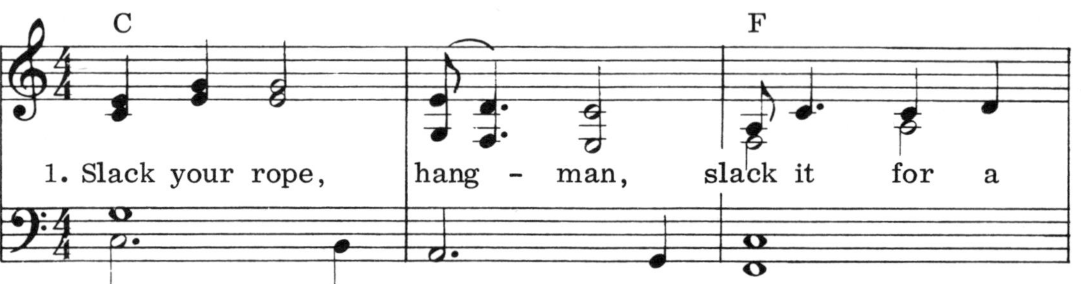

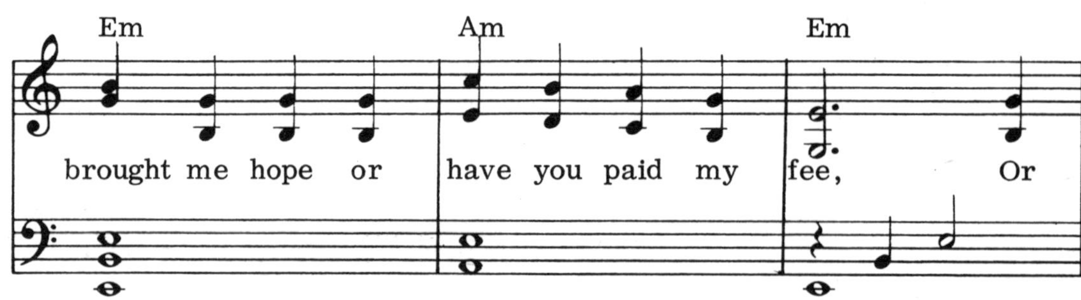

traditional

30 Whiskey in the jar

1 As I was going over Kilgary Mountain
I met with Captain Farrell and his money he was counting.
First I drew my pistol, and then I drew my sabre, saying
"Stand and deliver, for I am your bold deceiver."

Wi' my ring-um do-rum day,
Whack for the daddy-o,
Whack for my daddy-o,
There's whiskey in the jar.

2 He counted out his money and it made a pretty penny,
I loaded up and took it home and gave it to my Jenny.
She swore that she loved me, that she never would deceive me,
But the devil's in the women and they always lie so easy.
Wi' my ring-um do-rum day . . .

3 I woke next morning early, 'tween the hours of six and seven,
And the guards were standing round the bed in numbers odd and even.
I flew to my pistols but alas I was mistaken,
For Jenny'd wet the powder and a prisoner I was taken.
Wi' my ring-um do-rum day . . .

4 They threw me into Sligo jail with neither judge nor writing,
For robbing Captain Farrell as he crossed Kilgary Mountain,
But they didn't take my fists and so I knocked the jailer down,
And bid a distant farewell to the judge in Sligo Town.
Wi' my ring-um do-rum day . . .

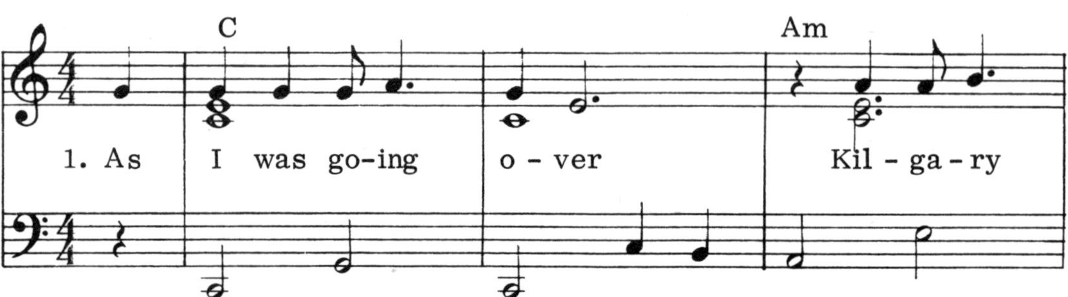

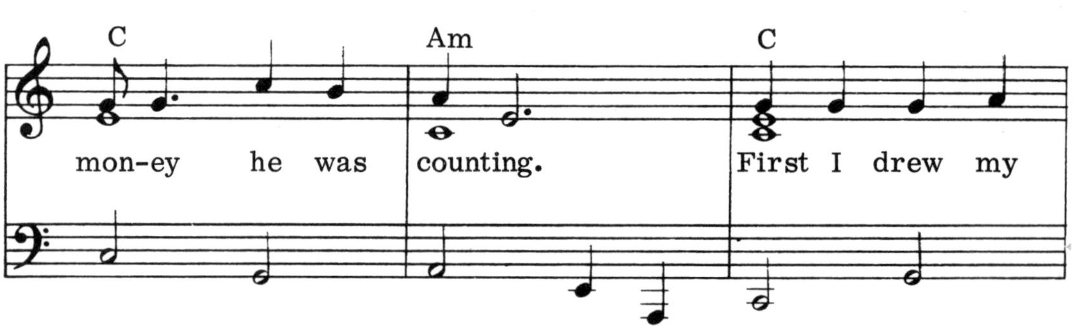

traditional

31 Turpin hero

1 As Turpin rode across the moor
He saw a lawyer riding before.
"Kind sir," says he, "aren't you afraid
Of Turpin, that mischievous blade?"

O rare Turpin hero,
O rare Turpin O.

2 Says Turpin, "He won't find me out,
I've hid my money in my boot."
The lawyer says, "No one can find
The gold stitched in my cape behind."

3 As they rode by the foot of the hill
Turpin commands him to stand still.
Says he, "Your cape I must cut off
For my mare she needs a new saddle-cloth."

4 As Turpin rode over Salisbury Plain
He met a judge with all his train.
Then to the judge he did approach
And robbed him as he sat in his coach.

5 For the shooting of a dunghill cock
Turpin now at last is took,
And now he lingers in a jail
Where his ill-luck he doth bewail.

6 Now Turpin is condemned to die
And hang upon the gallows high.
His legacy is the hangman's rope
For the shooting of a dunghill cock.

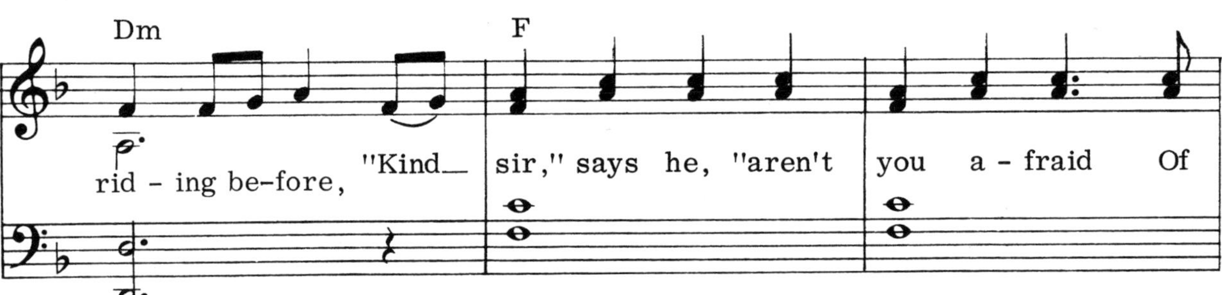

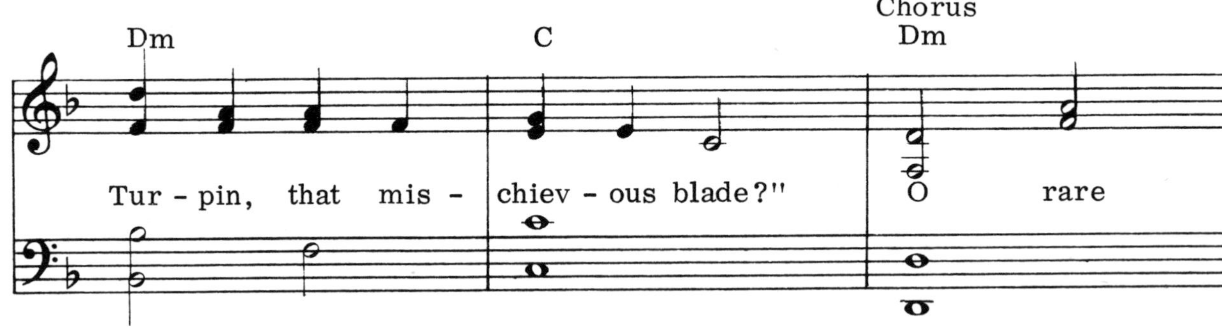

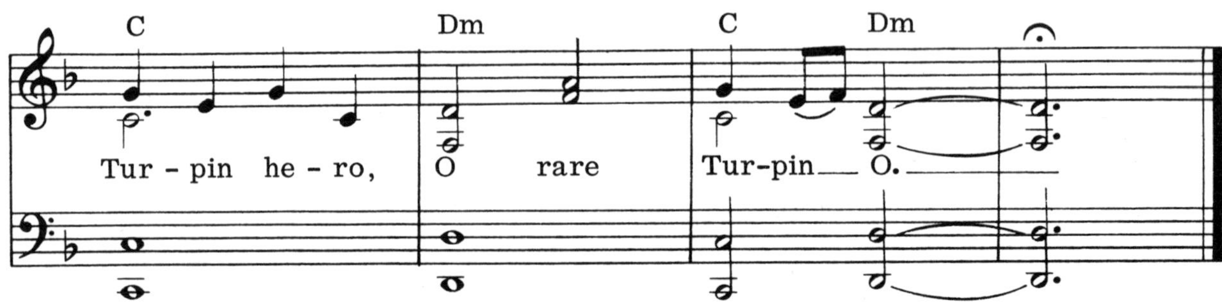

traditional

32 High Germany

1 Oh Polly, love, oh Polly,
the rout it is begun,
And we must march away
at the beating of the drum.
Go dress yourself all in your best
and come along with me,
I'll take you to the war, my love,
in High Germany.

2 Oh Billy, dearest Billy,
now mind what you do say,
My feet they are so tender
I cannot march away.
Besides, my dearest Billy,
I am with child by thee,
Not fitting for the cruel wars
in High Germany.

3 Cursed by the cruel wars
that ever they began,
For they have pressed my Billy
and many a clever man,
For they have pressed my Billy
and all my brothers three
And sent them to the cruel wars
in High Germany.

"High" Germany is Southern Germany

traditional

33 The bonnie lass o' Fyvie

1 There was a troop of Irish dragoons
Came marching down through Fyvie O,
And their captain fell in love with a handsome serving-maid
And her name it was called pretty Peggy O.

There's many a bonnie lass in the howe of Auchterless,
There's many a bonnie lass in the Garioch O,
There's many a bonnie Jean in the town o' Aberdeen,
But the flower of them all is in Fyvie O.

2 "Oh, it's come down the stair, pretty Peggy, my dear,
Come down the stair, pretty Peggy O.
Oh, come down the stair, comb back your yellow hair,
Take a last farewell o' your daddy O."

3 "A soldier's wife I never shall be.
A soldier shall never enjoy me O.
For I never do intend to go to a foreign land,
So I never shall marry a soldier O."

4 "A soldier's wife ye never shall be
For ye'll be the captain's lady O.
And the regiment shall stand with their hats into their hands
And they'll bow in the presence o' my Peggy O.

5 "It's braw, aye it's braw a captain's lady for to be.
It's braw to be a captain's lady O.
It's braw to rant and rove, and to follow at his word,
And to march when your captain he is ready O."

6 But the Colonel he cries, "Now mount, boys, mount."
The captain he cries, "Tarry O!
Oh, gang nae awa' for another day or twa
Till we see if this bonnie lass will marry O."

7 It was early next morning that we marched away
And oh, but our captain was sorry O.
The drums they did beat o'er the bonnie braes o' Gight
And the band played the Lowlands o' Fyvie O.

8 Long ere we won, into old Meldrum town
We had our captain to carry O.
And long ere we won, into bonnie Aberdeen
We had our captain to bury O.

9 Green grow the birks on bonnie Ythanside
And low lie the lowlands o' Fyvie O.
Our captain's name was Ned, and he died for a maid.
He died for the bonnie lass o' Fyvie O.

howe: area
Auchterless: pronounced Ochterless
Garioch: pronounced Geerie
braw: grand
braes: hills
birk: silver birch
Ythanside: pronounced eye-thanside

Steady march
G
1. There was a troop of I - rish dragoons came
D
march - ing down through Fy - vie O, And their
G C
cap-tain fell in love with a handsome serving maid, and her
D (C) G
name it was called pret - ty Peg - gy O.
traditional

34 John Barleycorn

1 There were three men came out of the west,
Their fortunes for to try,
And these three men made a solemn vow,
John Barleycorn should die.
They ploughed, they sowed, they harrowed him in,
Throwed clods upon his head,
And these three men made a solemn vow,
John Barleycorn was dead.

2 Then they let him lie for a very long time
Till the rain from heaven did fall,
Then little Sir John sprung up his head,
And soon amazed them all.
They let him stand till midsummer
Till he looked both pale and wan,
And little Sir John he growed a long beard
And so became a man.

3 They hired men with the scythes so sharp
To cut him off at the knee,
They rolled him and tied him by the waist,
And served him most barbarously.
They hired men with the sharp pitchforks
Who pricked him to the heart,
And the loader he served him worse than that,
For he bound him to the cart.

capo on 5th fret

G Am C

1. There— were three—men came out of the west, their—

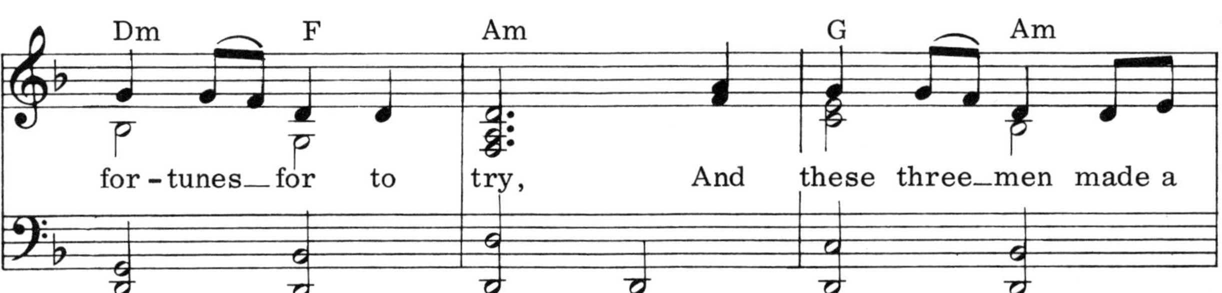

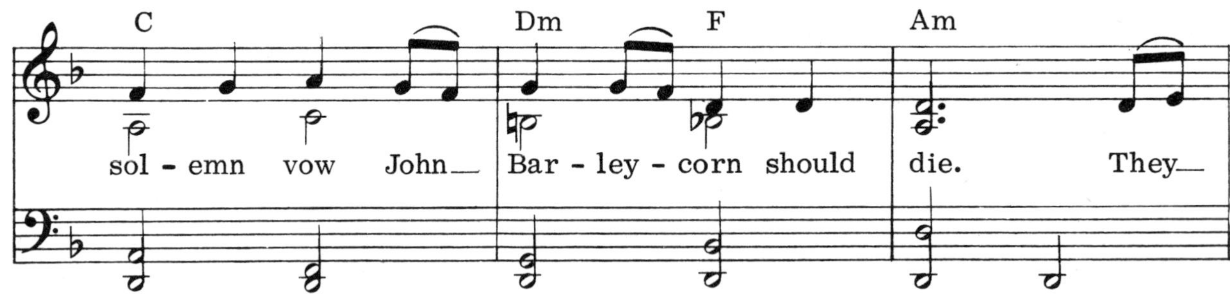

traditional

4 They wheeled him round and round the field
Till they came unto a barn,
And there they made a solemn mow
Of poor John Barleycorn.
They hired men with the crab-tree sticks
To cut him skin from bone,
And the miller he served him worse than that,
For he ground him between two stones.

5 Here's little Sir John in a nut-brown bowl,
And brandy in a glass;
And little Sir John in the nut brown bowl
Proved the stronger man at last.
And the huntsman he can't hunt the fox,
Nor so loudly blow his horn,
And the tinker he can't mend kettles or pots
Without a little of Barleycorn.

35 Casey Jones

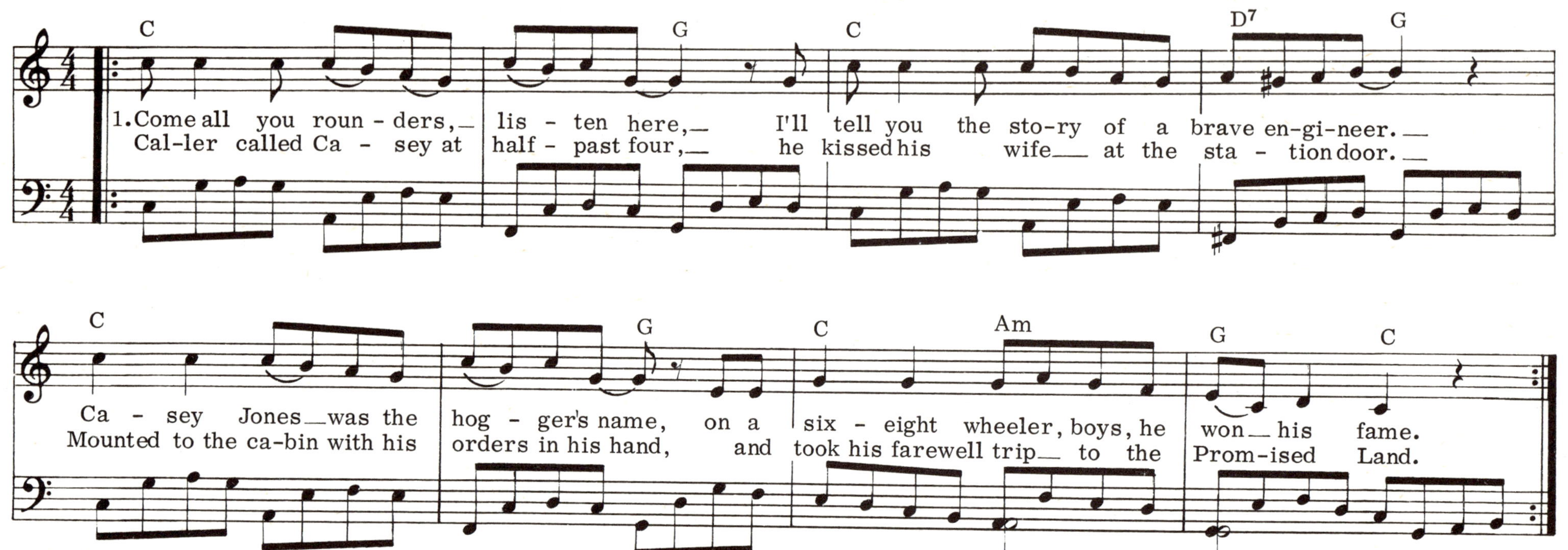

1 Come all you rounders, listen here,
I'll tell you the story of a brave engineer.
Casey Jones was the hogger's name,
On a six-eight wheeler, boys, he won his fame.

Caller called Casey at half-past four,
He kissed his wife at the station door,
Mounted to the cabin with his orders in his hand
And took his farewell trip to the Promised Land.

> Casey Jones! mounted to the cabin,
> Casey Jones! with his orders in his hand,
> Casey Jones! mounted to the cabin
> And took his farewell trip to the Promised
> Land.

2 Put in your water and shovel in your coal,
Put your head out the window, watch the drivers roll.
"I'll run her till she leaves the rail
'Cause we're eight hours late with the Western Mail."

He looked at his watch and his watch was slow,
Looked at the water and the water was low,
Turned to his fireboy, then he said,
"We're bound to reach Frisco but we'll all be dead."

> Casey Jones! bound to reach Frisco
> Casey Jones! but we'll all be dead,
> Casey Jones! bound to reach Frisco,
> We're bound to reach Frisco but we'll all be
> dead.

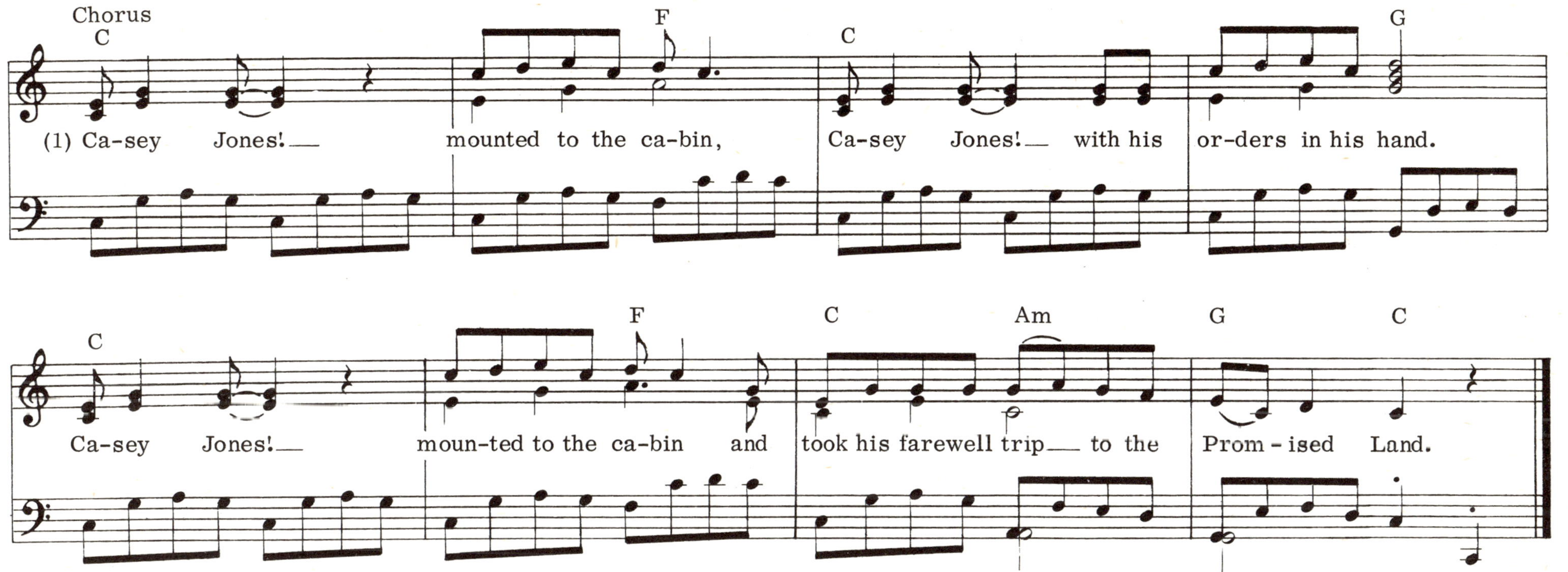

words: T. Lawrence Seibert
music: Eddie Newton

3 Casey pulled up Reno Hill,
Tooted at the crossing with an awful shrill.
"Snakes" all knew by the engine's moans
That the hogger at the throttle was Casey Jones.

He pulled up short two miles from the place,
Freight train stared him straight in the face,
Turned to his fireboy, "Son, you'd better jump
'Cause there's two locomotives that are going to bump."

Casey Jones! two locomotives
Casey Jones! that are going to bump,
Casey Jones! two locomotives,
There's two locomotives that are going to bump.

4 Casey said just before he died,
"There's two more roads I'd like to ride."
Fireboy asked, "What can they be?"
"The Rio Grande and the Santa Fe."

Mrs Jones sat on her bed a-sigh'n,
Had a pink that her Casey was dy'n,
Said, "Hush you children, stop your cry'n
'Cause you'll get another Papa on the Salt Lake Line."

Casey Jones! get another Papa
Casey Jones! on the Salt Lake Line,
Casey Jones! get another Papa,
You'll get another Papa on the Salt Lake Line.

36 The Gypsy Davey

1 It was late last night when the squire came home
And asking for his lady.
The only answer that he got,
"She's gone with the Gypsy Davey."

2 "Go saddle me my buckskin horse
And a hundred dollar saddle.
Point out to me their wagon tracks
And after them I'll travel."

3 Well, he had not rode to the midnight moon
When he saw the campfire gleaming.
He heard the noise of the big guitar
And the noise of the gypsies singing.

4 "Have you forsaken your horse and home?
Have you forsaken your baby?
Have you forsaken your husband dear
To go with the Gypsy Davey?"

5 "Yes, I've forsaken my husband dear
To go with the Gypsy Davey,
And I've forsaken my mansion high
But not my blue-eyed baby."

6 "Take off, take off your buckskin gloves
Made of Spanish leather,
Give to me your lily-white hand
And we'll ride home together."

7 "No, I won't take off my buckskin gloves
Made of Spanish leather.
I'll go my way from day to day
And sing with the Gypsy Davey."

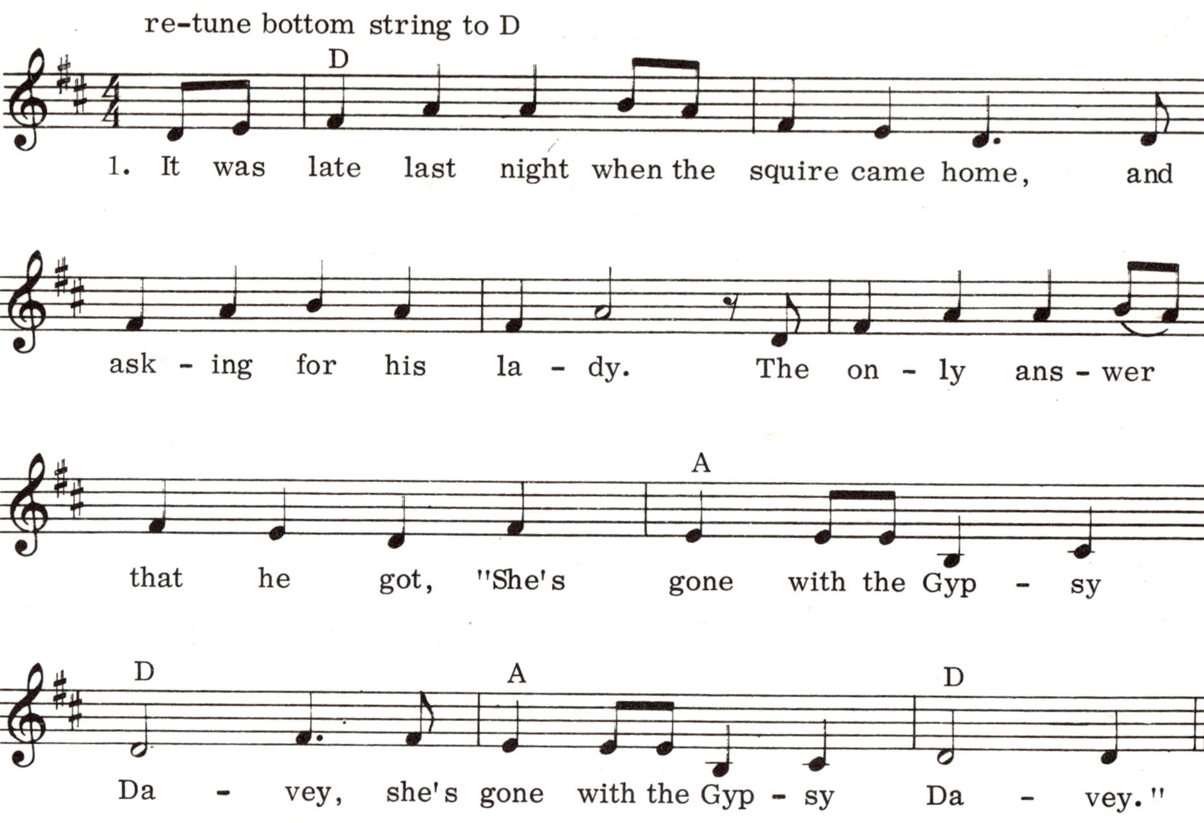

traditional

37 The gypsy rover

1 The gypsy rover came over the hill,
Bound for the valley so shady,
He whistled and sang till the
greenwoods rang,
And he won the heart of a lady.

Ah-di-do ah-di-do-da-day,
Ah-di-do ah-di-day-dee,
He whistled and sang till
the greenwoods rang,
And he won the heart of a lady.

2 She left her father's castle gate,
She left her own true lover,
She left her servants and her estate
To follow the gypsy rover.

3 Her father saddled his fastest steed,
Roamed the valley all over,
Sought his daughter at great speed,
And the whistling gypsy rover.

4 He came at last to a castle gate
Down by the river Claydie,
And there was whisky and there
was wine
For the gypsy and his lady.

5 He is no gypsy, father dear,
But lord of these lands all over,
And I will stay till my dying day
With my whistling gypsy rover.

The additional melody part is for recorder (descant or treble) or flute. Two recorders or two flutes can play a duet, one playing the upper part and the other playing the tune.

words and music: Leo Maguire

38 The Ellen Vannin Tragedy

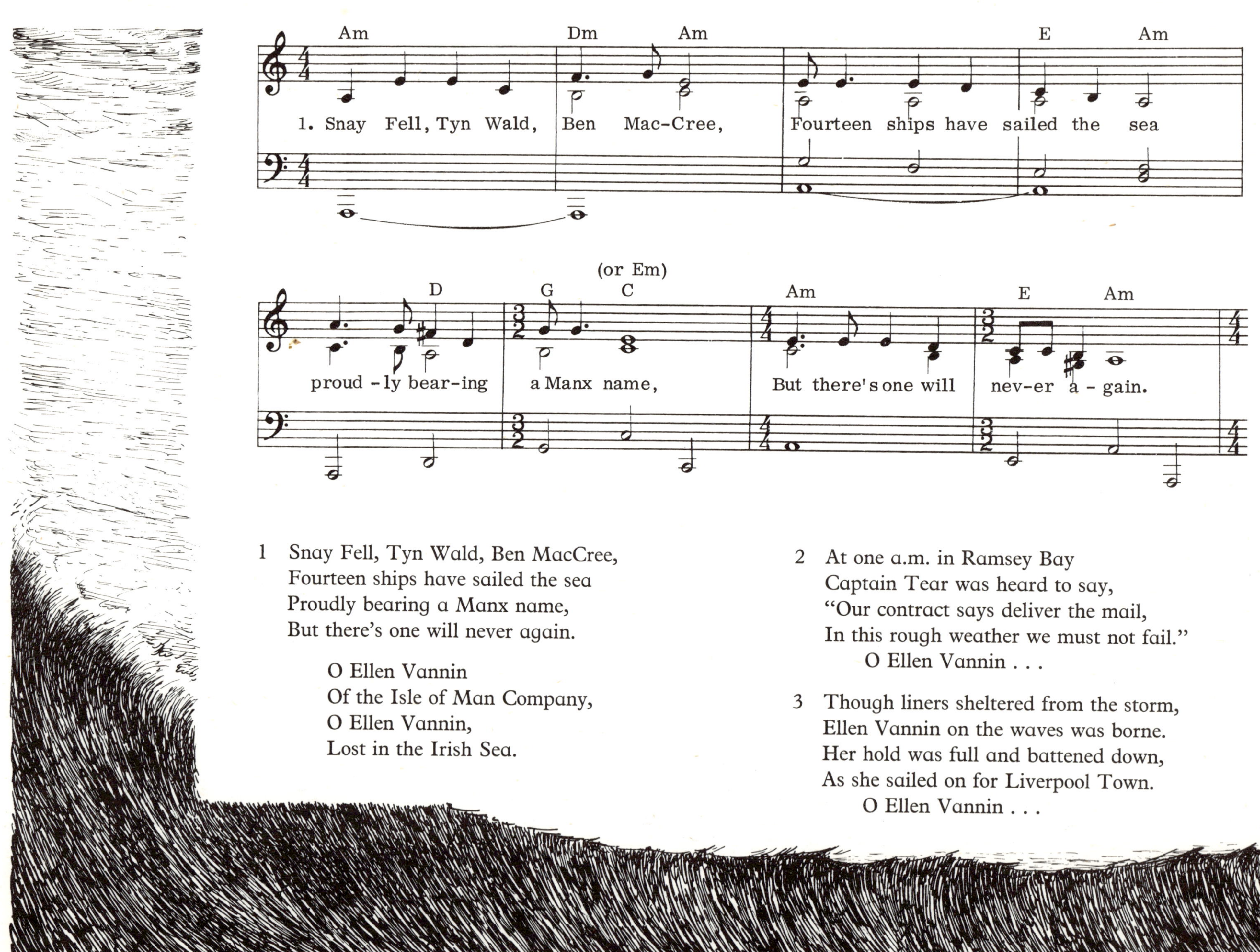

1 Snay Fell, Tyn Wald, Ben MacCree,
Fourteen ships have sailed the sea
Proudly bearing a Manx name,
But there's one will never again.

O Ellen Vannin
Of the Isle of Man Company,
O Ellen Vannin,
Lost in the Irish Sea.

2 At one a.m. in Ramsey Bay
Captain Tear was heard to say,
"Our contract says deliver the mail,
In this rough weather we must not fail."
O Ellen Vannin . . .

3 Though liners sheltered from the storm,
Ellen Vannin on the waves was borne.
Her hold was full and battened down,
As she sailed on for Liverpool Town.
O Ellen Vannin . . .

words and music: Hugh Jones

4 Less than a mile from the Bar lightship
By a mighty wave Ellen Vannin was hit.
She sank in the waters of Liverpool Bay,
And there she lies until this day.
O Ellen Vannin . . .

39 Dorset is beautiful

Dorset is beautiful wherever you go,
And the rain in the summertime
makes the wurzel tree grow.
And it's pleasant to sit
in the thunder and the hail,
With your girlfriend on a turnip stump
and hear the sweet nightingale.

1 As I was a-walking one evening in June
I spied two old farmers making hay in the moon.
Said one to the other with a twinkle in his eye,
"There be more birds in the long grass
than there be in the sky."
Dorset is beautiful . . .

2 Now Sarah's my girlfriend and I loves her so,
Her's as big as an 'aystack and forty years old.
Farmer says she's gi-normous, and loud do he scoff,
'Cos you has to leave a chalk-mark
to show where you left off.
Dorset is beautiful . . .

3 Farmer looks at young Gwendoline and then looks at Ned,
"What an 'andsome young couple, they ought to be wed."
But then he says sadly, "Tis impossible of course
'Cos Gwendoline's me daughter and Ned is me horse."
Dorset is beautiful . . .

4 When Sarah went milking with Nellie the cow
She pulled and she tugged but she didn't know quite
how,
So after a short while Nellie turned with a frown,
Said "You hang on tight, love, I'll jump up and down."
Dorset is beautiful . . .

Verse and chorus

D G A D

(chorus) Dor - set is beau-ti-ful wher - e-ver you go, and the

A

rain in the summer-time makes the wur - zel tree grow, —

D A

— and it's pleasant to sit — in the thunder and the hail, with your

D G A D

girl - friend on a tur - nip stump and hear the sweet night - in - gale. —

words: Robert Gale
music: Cantwell family

40 Fling it here, fling it there

1 Way down on our farm we are right up to date,
For mechanisation's the byword of late.
For every task there's a gadget to match,
But our new muck-spreader's the best of the batch.

Fling it here, fling it there,
If you're standing by then you'll all get
your share.

2 Now young Walter Hodgkins he brought back a load
Of liquid manure from the farm up the road.
He hummed to himself as he drove up the street,
And his load also hummmmmmed in the afternoon
heat.

3 Now this muck-spreader had a mechanical fault,
And a bump in the road turned it on with a jolt.
An odorous spray of manure it let fly
Without fear or favour on all who passed by.

C G (C)
1. Way down on our farm we are right up to

C D
date, For me - chan - i - za - tion's the

G C
by - word of late. For e - ve - ry

F C
task there's a gad-get to match, But

words and music: S. Lawrence/the Yetties

4 The cats and the dogs stank to high kingdom come,
And the kiddies, browned off, ran home screaming to Mum,
The trail of sheer havoc were terrible grim,
One open car were filled up to the brim.

5 The vicarage windows were all open wide
When a generous helping descended inside.
The vicar, at table, intoned "Let us pray"
When this manure from heaven came flying his way.

6 In her garden, Miss Pringle was quite scandalised.
"Good gracious!" she cried, "I've been fertilised."
While the Methodist minister's teetotal wife
Were plastered for the very first time in her life.

7 And all of this time Walter trundled along,
He was quite unaware there was anything wrong,
Till a vision of woe flagged him down —— what a sight!
A policeman all covered in . . . you've got it right.

41 Green lanes

Follow the old green lanes.
As the crow flies, so will I.
See how the grey stone walls
Climb the fell and try to touch the sky.

> Farms and cottages
> Clinging to the fellside,
> Far below us and in another world.

Travel the ancient ways
With only sheep to watch you.
See how the water tumbles
Down the fell and disappears from view.

> Come travel with me
> If the spirit moves you.
> Time's an illusion, so leave it far behind.

Follow the old green lanes.
As the crow flies, so will I.
See how the grey stone walls
Climb the fell and try to touch the sky.

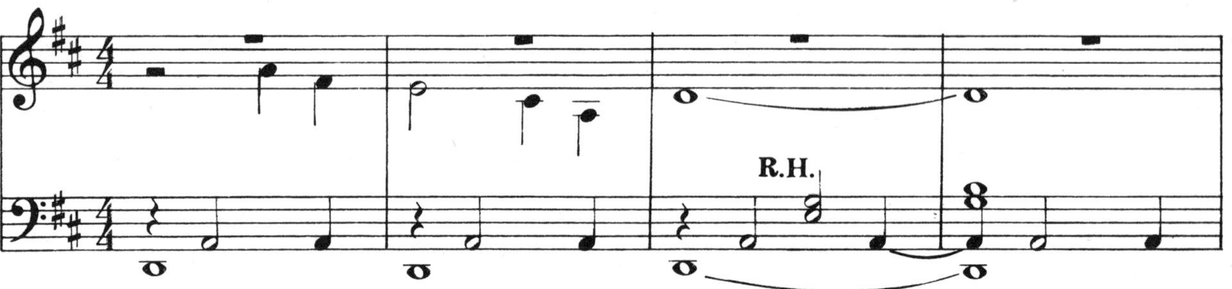

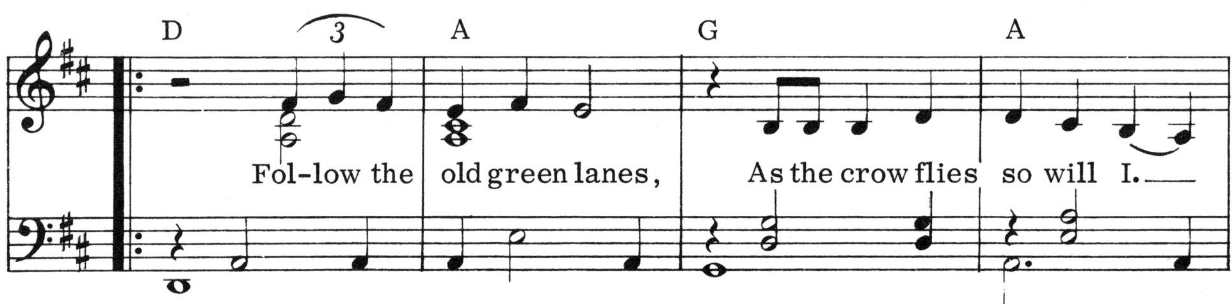

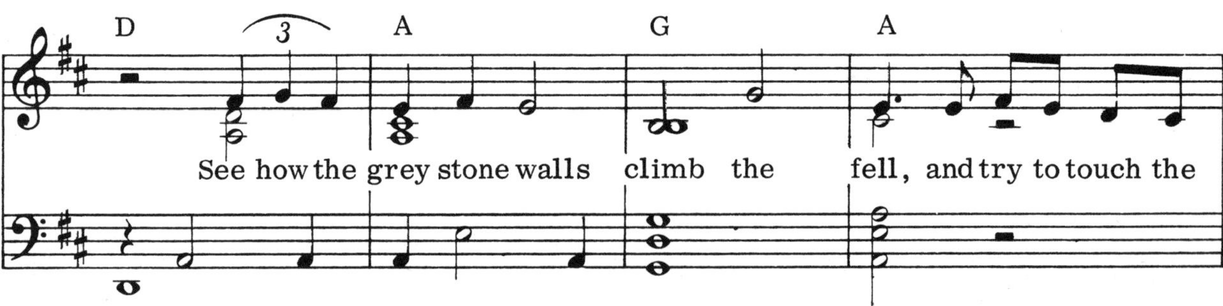

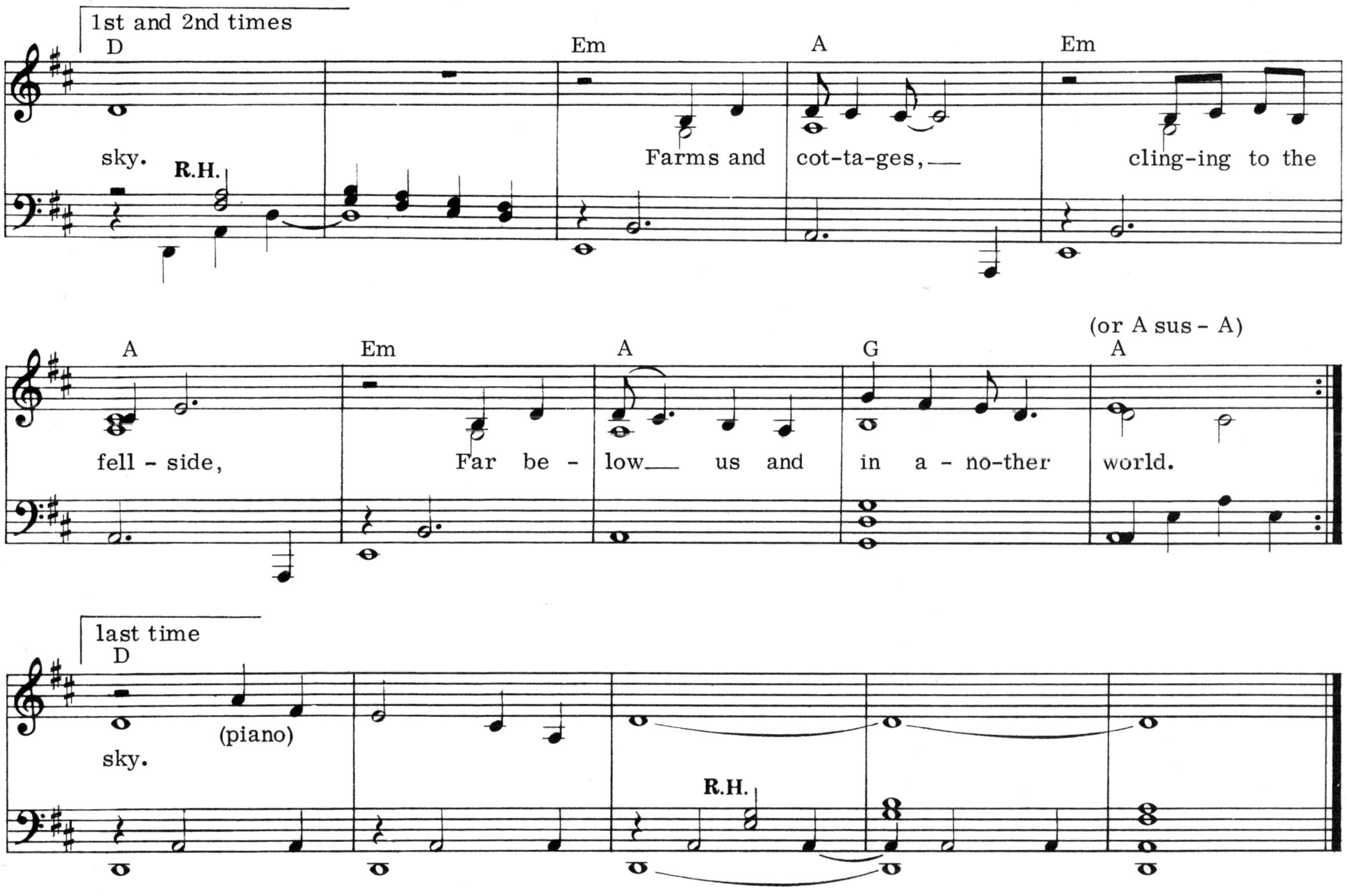

1st and 2nd times
D
Em
A
Em
sky.
R.H.
Farms and
cot-ta-ges,
cling-ing to the
A
Em
A
G
(or A sus - A)
A
fell - side,
Far be -
low
us and
in a - no-ther
world.
last time
D
(piano)
sky.
R.H.

words and music: Judith Bush

A sus
A

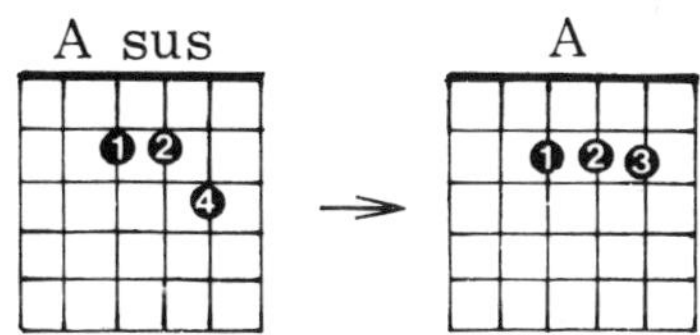

42 Land of the old and grey

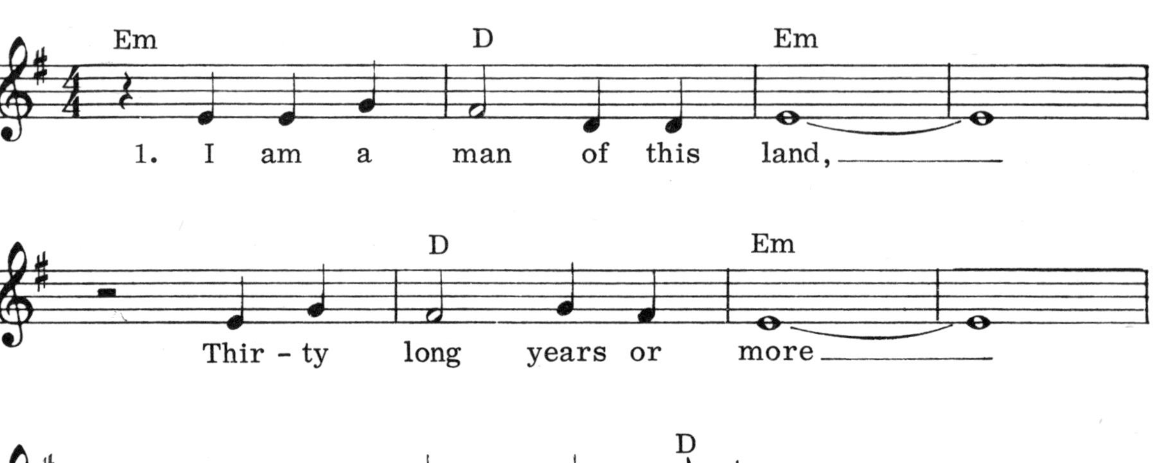

1 I am a man of this land,
Thirty long years or more
I have worked the Mallerstang Fells,
Never asked for more.

Young folks keep moving away,
Who can get them to stay?
There's money and there's jobs
in the wool towns of the valleys.
This is the land of the old and grey.

2 I have been a leadminer
Over the Swaledale way.
The clothes on your back, they never get dry,
Freezing on a winter's day.
Young folks keep moving away . . .

3 I have seen the colours of this land,
Thirty long years or more.
Many men drifting to the mines of Durham,
To the Bradford factory floor.
Young folks keep moving away . . .

4 Working on the Carlisle railway
Mending broken track.
There's snow on the fells and it's raining
in the valleys,
Muscles aching in my back.
Young folks keep moving away . . .

words and music: Mike Donald

43 If it wasn't for the 'ouses in between

words: Edgar Bateman *music: George le Brunn*

44 The drunken sailor

1 What shall we do with the drunken sailor,
What shall we do with the drunken sailor,
What shall we do with the drunken sailor,
Early in the morning?

Hooray and up she rises,
Hooray and up she rises,
Hooray and up she rises,
Early in the morning.

2 Put him in the longboat till he's sober . . .

3 Hoist him aboard with a running bowline . . .

4 Put him in the scuppers with a hosepipe on him . . .

5 Pull out the plug and wet him all over . . .

6 Shave his belly with a rusty razor . . .

7 That's what we do with the drunken sailor . . .

traditional (windlass and capstan shanty)

45 Can't you dance the polka

1 As I walked down the Broadway
  one evening in July,
I met a girl, she asked my trade,
  a sailor John says I.

Then away, you Santee, my dear Annie,
Oh you New York gals, can't you dance
  the polka?

2 To Tiffany's I took her,
  I did not mind expense,
I bought her two gold earrings,
  they cost me fifteen cents.
Then away, you Santee, my dear Annie . . .

3 Says she "You Limejuice sailor,
  now see me home you may."
But when we reached her cottage door,
  she unto me did say,
Then away, you Santee, my dear Annie . . .

4 "My flashman he's a Yankee
  with his hair cut short behind,
He wears a tarry jumper
  and he sails in the Black Ball Line."
Then away, you Santee, my dear Annie . . .

traditional (capstan shanty)

46 Haul away Joe

traditional (short-haul shanty)

In shanties like *Haul away Joe* and *Santy Anna* a leader or shantyman would have sung the first and third lines, with the rest of the sailors singing the unchanging second and fourth lines.

1 Way, haul away, we'll haul away together,
   Way, haul away, we'll haul away Joe,
Way, haul away, we'll haul for better weather,
   Way, haul away, we'll haul away Joe.

2 Now when I was a little lad me mother always told me
   Way, haul away, we'll haul away Joe,
That if I didn't kiss the girls my lips would go all mouldy,
   Way, haul away, we'll haul away Joe.

3 Once I had a German girl and she was fat and lazy
And next I had an Irish girl, she damn near drove me crazy.

4 King Louis was the king of France before the revolution,
King Louis got his head cut off and spoiled his constitution.

5 Once I had a scolding wife, she wasn't very civil,
I clapped a plaster on her mouth and sent her to the divil.

6 Way, haul away, we'll haul for better weather.
Way, haul away, we'll haul and hang together.

47 Santy Anna

capo on 5th fret

1 Oh Santy Anna won the day
Hooray, Santy Anna!
And General Taylor ran away
All on the plains of Mexico.

2 He beat the Prooshans fairly
Hooray, Santy Anna!
And whacked the British nearly
All on the plains of Mexico.

3 He was a rorty general
Hooray, Santy Anna!
A rorty snorty general
All on the plains of Mexico.

4 Twas on the field of Molly del Rey
Hooray, Santy Anna!
Santy Anna lost a leg that day
All on the plains of Mexico.

5 Oh Santy Anna's dead and gone
Hooray, Santy Anna!
And all the fighting has been done
All on the plains of Mexico.

6 So heave away for Mexico
Hooray, Santy Anna!
For Mexico where the whalefish blow
All on the plains of Mexico.

"Santy Anna" is Antonio Lopez de Santa Anna (1795-1876), a Mexican general who led a highly eventful military and political life during which he was twice made President of Mexico. He was a popular hero to the sailors, and appears in several of their songs, notably this very fine capstan and windlass shanty.

traditional (windlass and capstan shanty)

48 The leaving of Liverpool

1 Fare thee well, the Prince's Landing Stage,
River Mersey, fare thee well,
For I'm bound for Californiay,
A place that I know well.

So fare thee well, my own true love,
When I return united we will be.
It's not the leaving of Liverpool that grieves me
But darling when I think of thee.

2 Yes I'm bound for Californiay
By way of the stormy Cape Horn,
But you know I'll write to you a letter,
My love, when I am homeward bound.
So fare thee well, my own true love . . .

3 I have signed on a Yankee clipper ship,
Davy Crockett is her name,
And her captain's name, it is Burgess,
And they say she's a floating shame.
So fare thee well, my own true love . . .

4 It's my second trip with Burgess in the *Crockett*,
And I reckon to know him well.
If a man is a sailor then he'll be all right,
But if not, why he's sure in hell.
So fare thee well, my own true love . . .

5 Oh the tug is waiting at the Pier Head
To take us down the stream,
Our sails are loose and the anchor is stowed,
So fare thee well again.
So fare thee well, my own true love . . .

6 Farewell to Lower Frederick Street,
Anson Terrace and Park Lane,
For I know that it's going to be a long, long time
Before I see you again.
So fare thee well, my own true love . . .

G F C

fare thee well, my own true___ love, When

G

I re-turn u-ni-ted we will be.________ It's not the

C F C

leav-ing of Li-ver-pool that grieves________ me, But___

G C

dar-ling when I think of thee.

traditional

49 The Marco Polo

1 The *Marco Polo*'s a very fine ship,
The fastest on the sea.
On Australia's sand we soon will land,
Bully Forbes can look for me.
Gonna jump this ship in Melbourne Town,
Go a-digging gold,
There's a fortune found beneath the ground
Where the eucalyptus grow.

Marco Polo, the fastest on the sea.

2 The Blackball owner Mr. Baines
Said to Bully Forbes one day
"It's up to you to keep your crew
When the gold calls them away."
Said Bully Forbes to Mr. Baines
"I have a plan so fine;
Leave it to me and you'll agree
I'm the king of the Blackball Line."

Marco Polo, the fastest on the sea.

3 Now when we reached the Australian shore
Bully Forbes he made this rule:
"There's scurvy, boys, so on board you'll stay
Till we're back in Liverpool."
And now we lie in the Salthouse Dock,
I'll go to sea no more.
I've done my time in the Blackball Line
Under Captain Bully Forbes.

Marco Polo, the fastest on the sea.

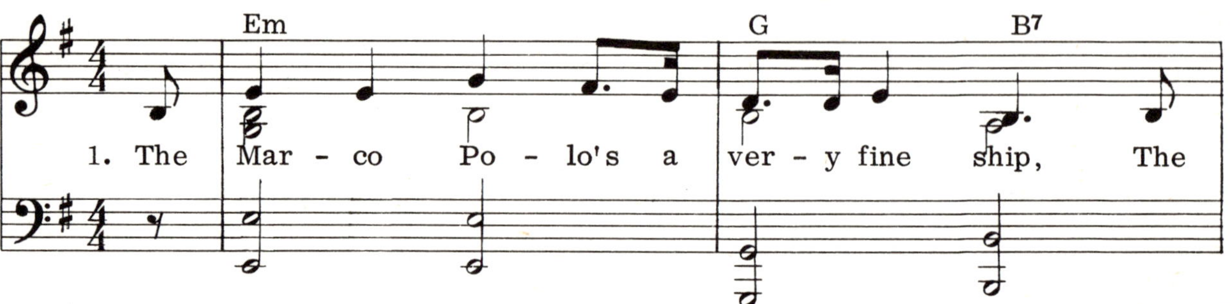

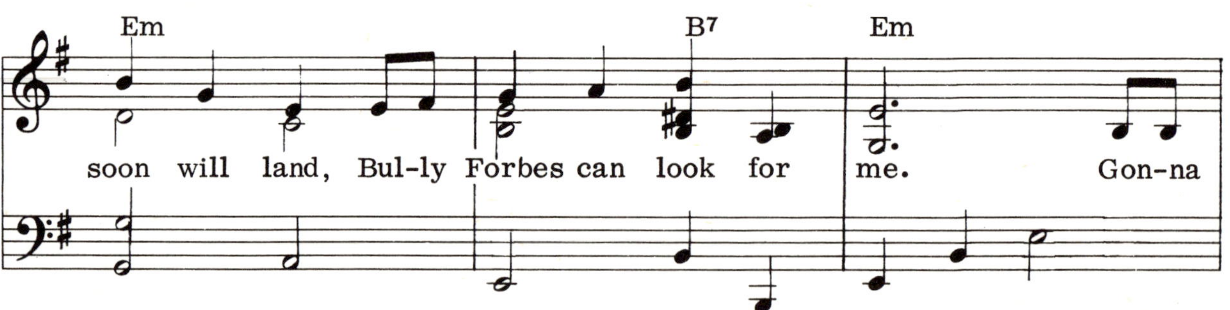

This song is about the Australian gold rush, which prompted many sailors to desert their ships in the hope of getting rich by finding gold. The *Marco Polo*, owned by the Blackball Company, sailed between Liverpool and Australia under the captaincy of James Forbes, known as Bully Forbes for his harsh treatment of the sailors. The song tells of one way he prevented them from deserting when they reached Australia.

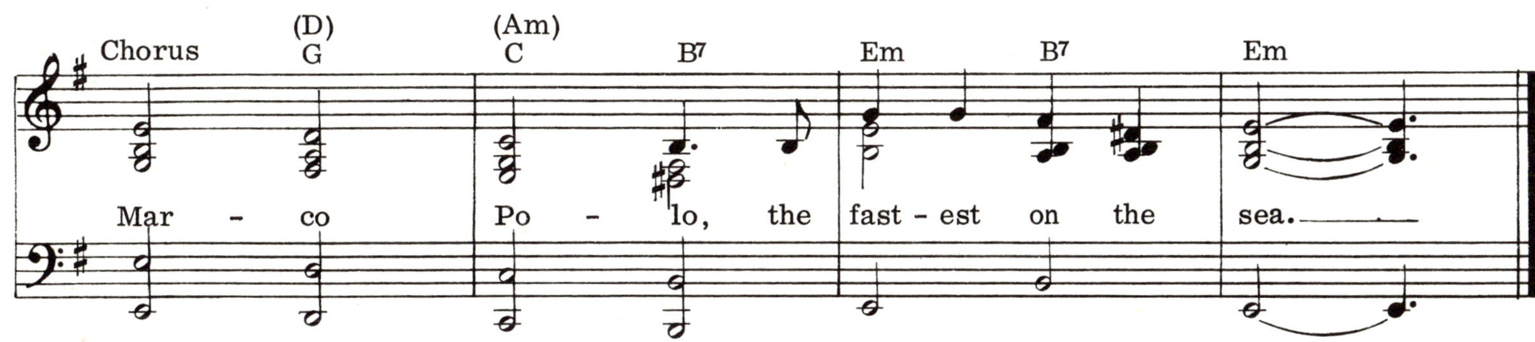

words and music: Hugh Jones

50 The wreck of the John B

1 We come on the sloop *John B*,
My grandfather and me,
Round Nassau town we did roam,
Drinking all night,
Got into a fight,
I feel so broke up, I wanna go home.

So hoist up the *John B*'s sails,
See how the main-sail sets,
Send for the captain ashore, let me go home,
I wanna go home,
Let me go home,
I feel so broke up, I wanna go home.

2 The first mate, he got drunk,
Broke up the people's trunk,
Constable had to come and take him away.
Sheriff John Stone,
Please let me alone,
I feel so broke up, I wanna go home.
So hoist up the *John B*'s sails . . .

traditional

51 Pay me my money down

leader and chorus: Pay me, O pay me,
Pay me my money down,
Pay me or go to jail,
Pay me my money down.

1 **leader:** I thought I heard our Captain say
chorus: Pay me my money down,
leader: Tomorrow is our sailing day.
chorus: Pay me my money down.

leader and chorus: Pay me, O pay me,
Pay me my money down,
Pay me or go to jail,
Pay me my money down.

2 The very next day we crossed the bar,
Pay me my money down,
He hit me on the head with an iron spar.
Pay me my money down.
Pay me, O pay me . . .

3 I wish I was Mr. Jackson's son,
Pay me my money down,
Sit on the fence and watch work done.
Pay me my money down.
Pay me, O pay me . . .

The chorus sections of this song may be sung in simple two-part harmony, using the arrangement given here. The piano accompanist might leave out the right hand as soon as the singers know their notes, and later leave them to sing completely unaccompanied.

The leader-and-chorus pattern suits many shanties and work-songs: *The drunken sailor*, *Can't you dance the polka*, *Haul away Joe* and *Santy Anna* were all originally leader-and-chorus songs.

traditional

52 Fulera mama

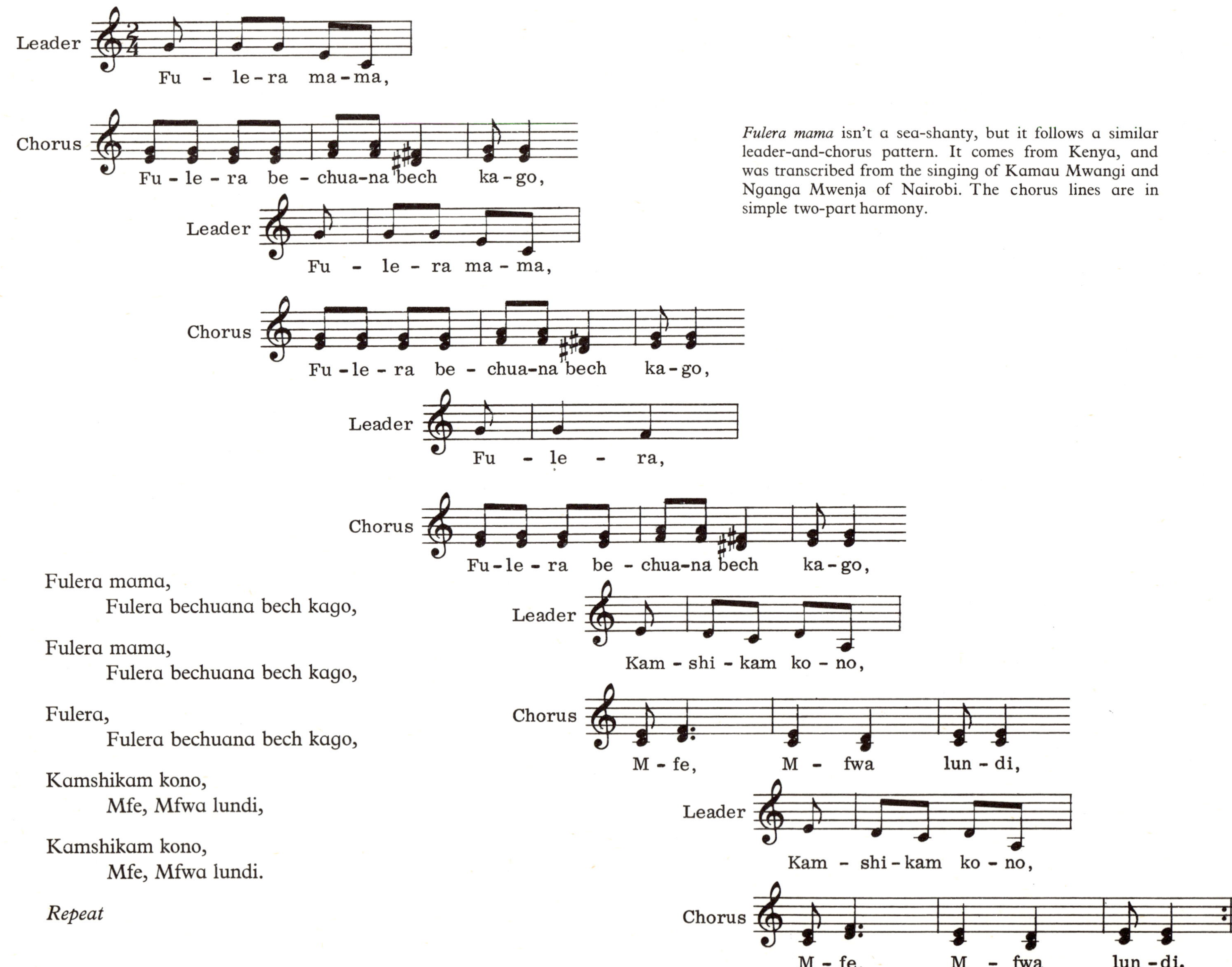

Fulera mama isn't a sea-shanty, but it follows a similar leader-and-chorus pattern. It comes from Kenya, and was transcribed from the singing of Kamau Mwangi and Nganga Mwenja of Nairobi. The chorus lines are in simple two-part harmony.

Fulera mama,
Fulera bechuana bech kago,

Fulera mama,
Fulera bechuana bech kago,

Fulera,
Fulera bechuana bech kago,

Kamshikam kono,
Mfe, Mfwa lundi,

Kamshikam kono,
Mfe, Mfwa lundi.

Repeat

53 Whip jamboree

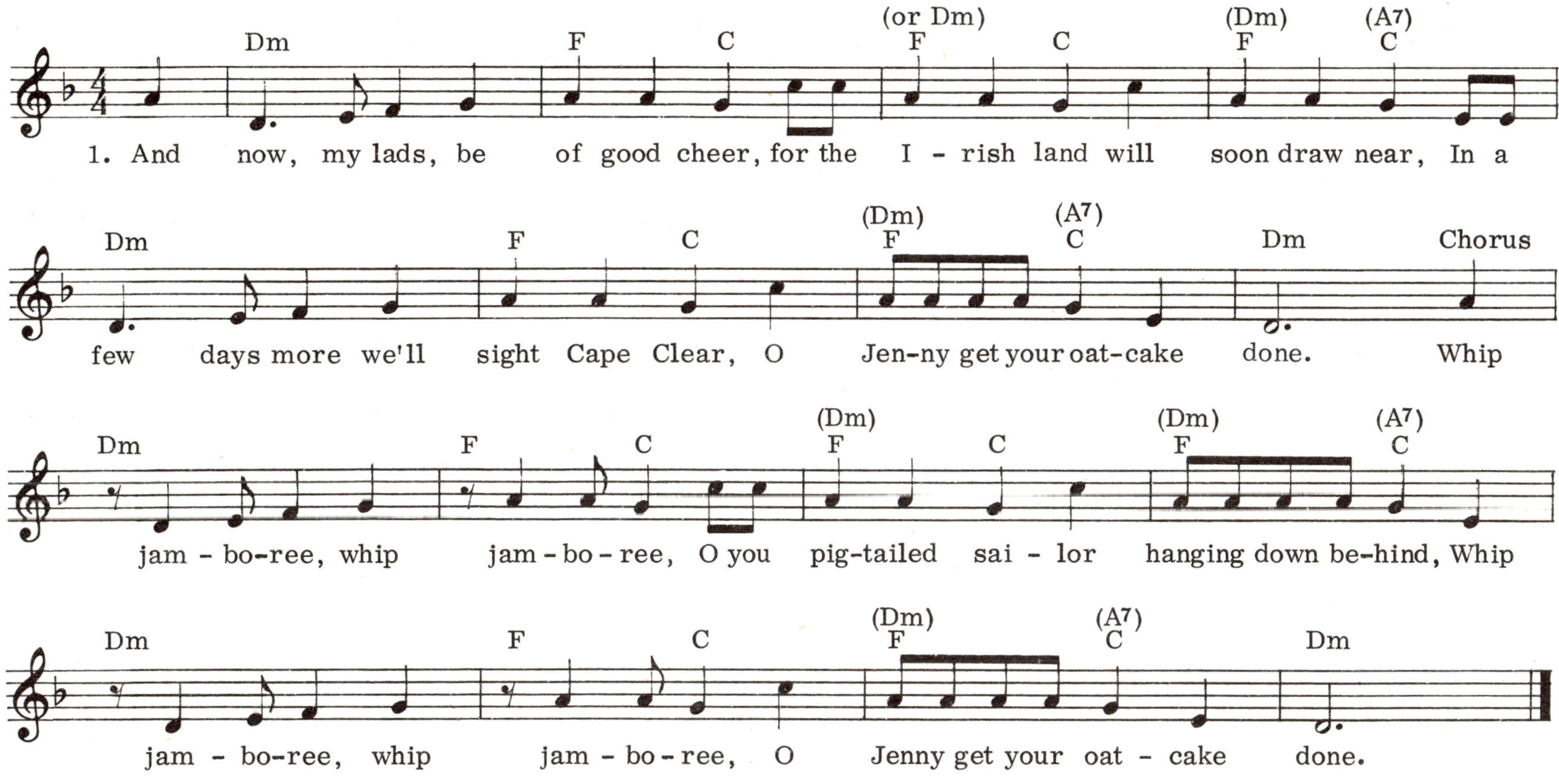

traditional

1 And now, my lads, be of good cheer,
For the Irish land will soon draw near.
In a few days more we'll sight Cape Clear,
O Jenny get your oat-cake done.

Whip jamboree, whip jamboree,
O you pigtailed sailor hanging down behind,
Whip jamboree, whip jamboree,
O Jenny get your oat-cake done.

2 And now Cape Clear it is in sight,
We'll be off Holyhead by tomorrow night,
And we'll shape our course for the old Rock Light,
O Jenny get your oat-cake done.
Whip jamboree, whip jamboree . . .

3 And now, my lads, we're round the Rock,
All hammocks lashed and chests all locked.
We'll haul her into Waterloo dock,
O Jenny get your oat-cake done.
Whip jamboree, whip jamboree . . .

54 The Curragh of Kildare

1 The winter it is past
And the summer's come at last,
And the birds they are singing in the trees;
Their little hearts are glad,
O but mine is very sad,
For my true love is far away from me.

> And straight I will repair
> To the Curragh of Kildare,
> For it's there I'll find tidings of my dear.

2 A livery I'll wear
And I'll comb back my hair,
And in velvet serene I will appear.
> And straight I will repair . . .

3 For you that are in love,
And it cannot remove,
I pity the pains that you endure;
For experience lets me know
That your hearts are full of woe,
A wound that no mortal can cure.
> And straight I will repair . . .

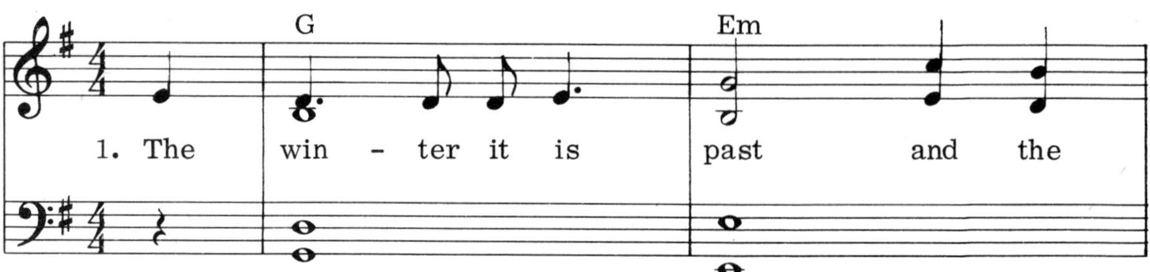

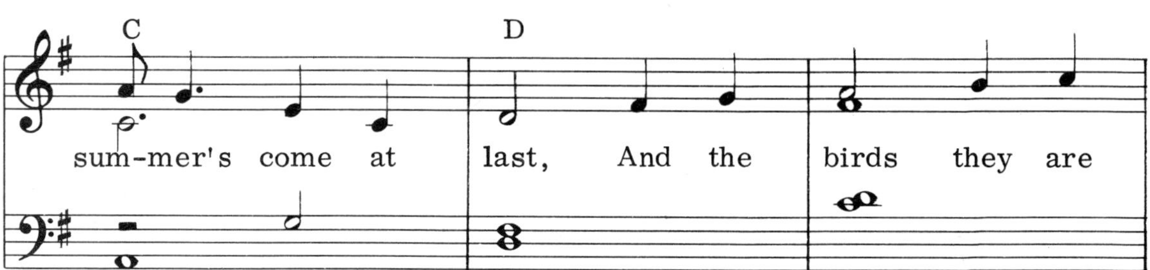

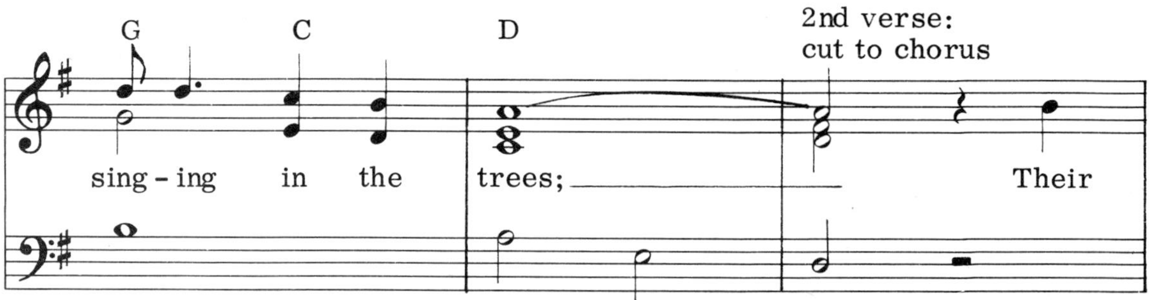

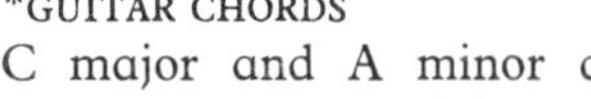
*GUITAR CHORDS
C major and A minor are closely related chords, often (though not always) interchangeable. This particular passage, which comes four times in the song, can be harmonised:

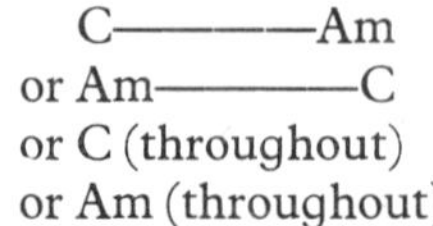
C———Am
or Am———C
or C (throughout)
or Am (throughout)

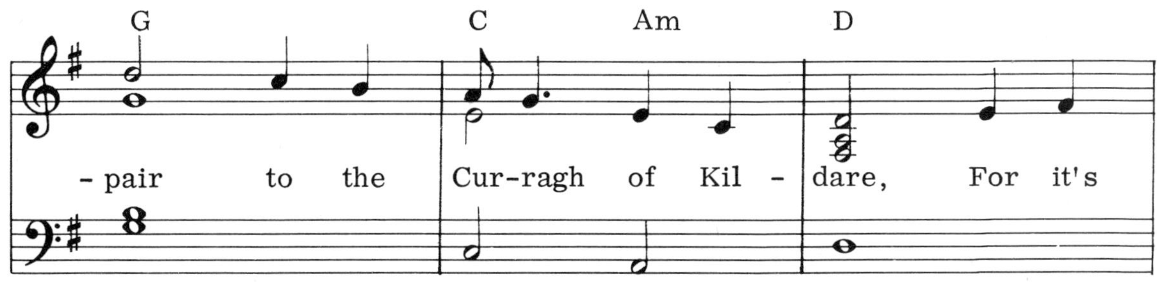

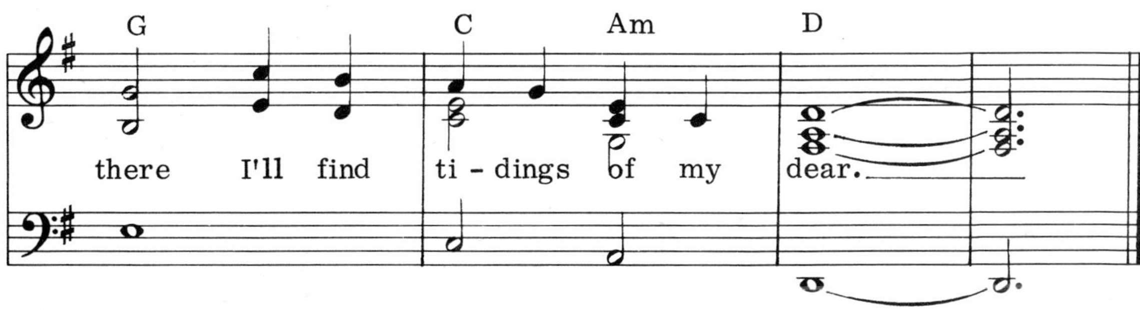

traditional

55 The girl I left behind

1 There was a wealthy old farmer
Who lived in the country nearby,
He had a lovely daughter
On whom I cast an eye,
She was pretty, tall and handsome,
Indeed, so very fair,
There was no other girl in the country
With her I could compare.

2 I asked her if she would be willing
For me to cross over the plains,
She said it would make no difference,
So I returned again,
She said that she would be true to me
Till death should prove unkind,
We kissed and then we parted,
I left my girl behind.

3 Out in a western city, boys,
A town we all know well,
Where everyone was friendly
And to show me all around,
Where work and money was plentiful
And the girls to me proved kind,
But the only object on my mind
Was the girl I left behind.

4 As I was rambling around one day
All down on the public square,
The mailcoach had arrived
And I met the mailboy there,
He handed to me a letter
That gave me to understand
That the girl I left in old Texas
Had married another man.

5 I turned myself all around and about,
Not knowing what else to do,
I read on down a piece further
To see if these words proved true.
It's drinking I throw over,
Card-playing I resign,
For the only girl that I ever loved
Was the girl I left behind.

6 Come all you rambling gambling boys,
And listen while I tell,
Does you no good, kind friends,
I am sure it will do you no harm,
If ever you court a fair young maid,
Just marry her while you can,
For if ever you cross over the plains,
She'll marry some other man.

capo on 5th fret
(or Em)
Am E7
1. There was a wealthy old far - mer who lived in the country near-
Am F C
- by, He had a love - ly daugh - ter on
(Am) E7 Am
whom I cast an eye. She was pret-ty, tall and
F C (Am) E7
hand - some, in - deed, so ver - y fair, There was
Am E7 Am
no o-ther girl in the coun - try with her I could com - pare.
traditional

56 Sweet Willie

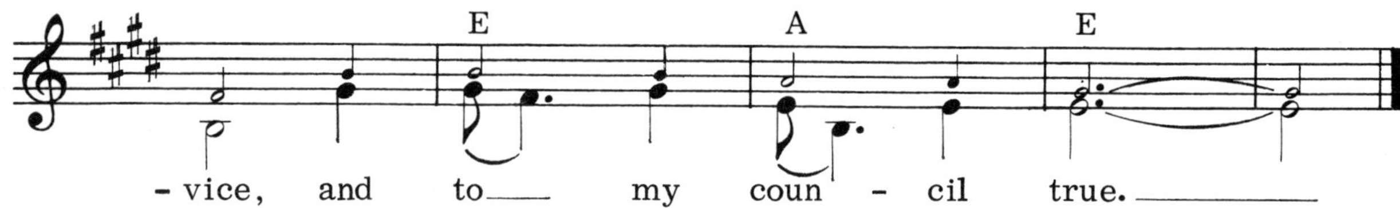

traditional, arranged by Jean Ritchie

The full-size notes are the main melody, and the small notes are for a second (harmonising) voice.

1 Come all young girls of a tender mind,
My story I'll tell to you,
And listen well to my advice,
And to my counsel true.

2 As a rule, the mind of a girl is weak
And the mind of a man is strong,
And if you listen to what they say
They're sure to lead you wrong.

3 When I was in my sixteenth year
Sweet Willie courted me,
He said if I'd run away with him
His loving bride I'd be.

4 I love my mother as my life,
I love my father well,
But the love I have for sweet Willie dear
No human tongue can tell.

5 When we were far away from home,
Enjoying a happy life,
He said "Go home, go home, little girl,
For you never can be my wife."

6 "O Willie dear, what have I done?
What makes you treat me so?
How can you take me from my home
And leave me here to mourn?"

7 "It's nature, nature, my little girl,
I find no fault in you;
My mind is set on rambling around,
And now I bid you adieu."

57 Handsome Molly

1 Wish I was in London
Or some other seaport town,
I'd set my foot in a steamboat,
I'd sail the ocean round.

2 While sailing around the ocean,
While sailing around the sea,
I'd think of handsome Molly
Wherever she might be.

3 She rode to church a-Sunday,
She passed me on by,
I saw her mind was changing
By the roving of her eye.

4 Don't you remember, Molly,
When you gave me your right hand?
You said if you ever marry
That I'd be the man.

5 Now you've broke your promise
Go marry who you please,
While my poor heart is aching
You're lying at your ease.

6 Hair was black as a raven,
Her eyes were black as coal,
Her cheeks were like lilies
That in the morning grow.

7 If I was in London
Or some other seaport town,
I'd set my foot in a steamboat,
I'd sail the ocean round.

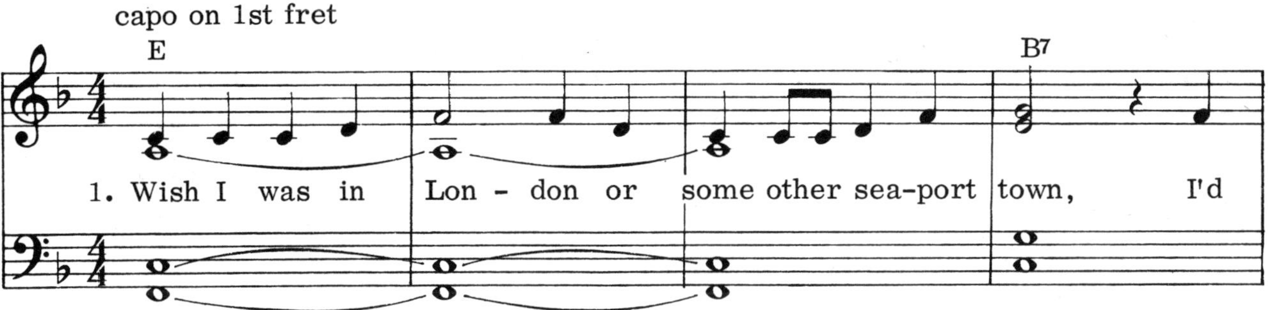

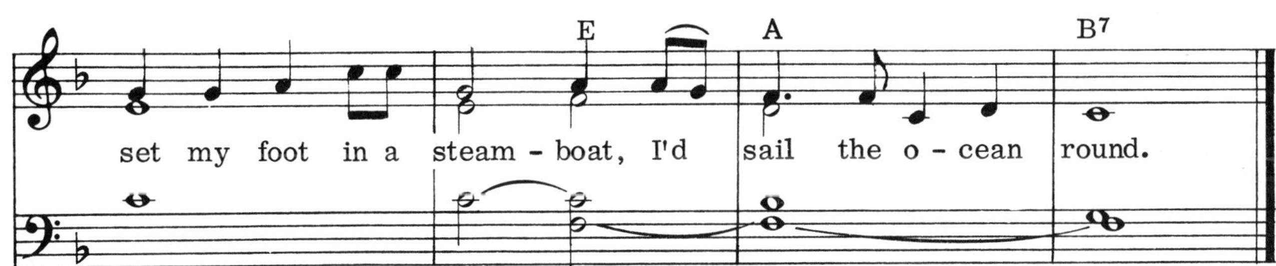

traditional

58 The water is wide

traditional

1 The water is wide, I cannot get o'er,
And neither have I wings to fly.
Give me a boat that will carry two,
And both shall row, my love and I.

2 Down in the meadow the other day,
A-gathering flowers both fine and gay,
A-gathering flowers both red and blue,
I little thought what love can do.

3 I leaned my back up against an oak,
Thinking that he was a trusty tree,
But first he bent and then he broke,
And so did my false love to me.

4 I put my hand into some soft bush,
Thinking the fairest flower to find;
I pricked my finger to the bone,
But O, I left the rose behind.

5 A ship there is, she sails the seas,
She's loaded deep as deep can be,
But not so deep as the love I'm in,
I know not if I sink or swim.

6 O love is handsome and love is fine
And love's a jewel while it is new,
But when it's old it groweth cold
And fades away like morning dew.

59 Once I had a sweetheart

1 Once I had a sweetheart but now I have none,
Once I had a sweetheart but now I have none.
He's gone and left me,
He's gone and left me,
He's gone and left me in sorrow to mourn.

2 Last night in sweet slumber I dreamed I did see,
Last night in sweet slumber I dreamed I did see
My own dearest jewel,
My own dearest jewel,
My own dearest jewel sat smiling by me.

3 And when I awakened and found it not so,
And when I awakened and found it not so,
My eyes, like some fountain,
My eyes, like some fountain,
My eyes, like some fountain, with tears overflowed.

4 I'll set sail for Dublin, for France and for Spain,
I'll set sail for Dublin, for France and for Spain
In hopes for to meet,
In hopes for to meet,
In hopes for to meet my dear jewel again.

traditional

60 Liverpool Lou

O Liverpool Lou, lovely Liverpool Lou,
Why don't you behave just like other girls do?
Why must my poor heart keep following you?
Stay home and love me, my Liverpool Lou.

1 When I go a-walking
I hear people talking,
School children playing,
I know what they're saying,
They're saying you'll grieve me,
That you will deceive me,
Some morning you'll leave me,
All packed up and gone.
O Liverpool Lou, lovely Liverpool Lou . . .

2 The sounds from the river
Keep telling me ever
That I should forget you
Like I'd never met you.
O tell me the song, love,
Was never more wrong, love,
Please say I belong, love,
To my Liverpool Lou.
O Liverpool Lou, lovely Liverpool Lou . . .

words and music: Dominic Behan

61 The orchestra song

violins: The violins of all the strings
We take the lead and have the most to do.
We gaily play the melody
And sing away the whole piece through.

clarinets: The clarinet, the clarinet
Of all the woodwind we most notes can get.
A single reed is all we need
To make our smooth and mellow sound.

horns: The horns, the horns
Of curling brass
Can murmur low
Or loudly blast.

trumpets: For the fanfare our trumpety sound is best,
Our trumpety sound is best, our trumpety
sound is best.
For the fanfare our trumpety sound is best,
Our trumpety sound is best, is best!

music: Willy Geissler
English words by John Hosier

drums: The kettle drums echo
The two notes we best know:
Soh, doh, doh soh,
Soh soh soh soh doh.

62 I'm not strong, Sir

three-part round

I'm not strong, Sir,
Sure, 'tis wrong, Sir,
Such high notes my voice do strain.

I can't sing a note, Sir,
Something hurts my throat, Sir,
Though I try my best, 'tis all in vain.

I'm quite hoarse, Sir,
So, of course, Sir,
I cannot sing this round again.

63 Have you seen the ghost of Tom?

four-part round

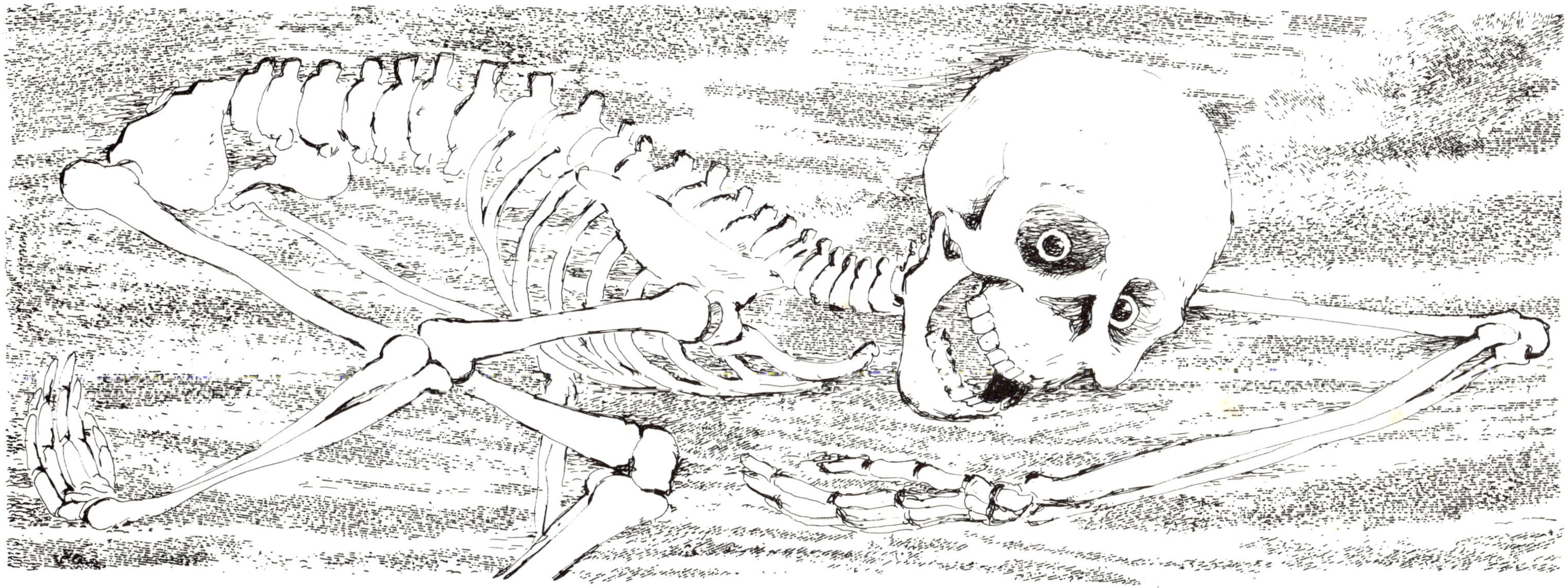

Have you seen the ghost of Tom?
Long white bones with the rest all gone,
Oooooooooooooooooooh,
Wouldn't it be chilly with no skin on?

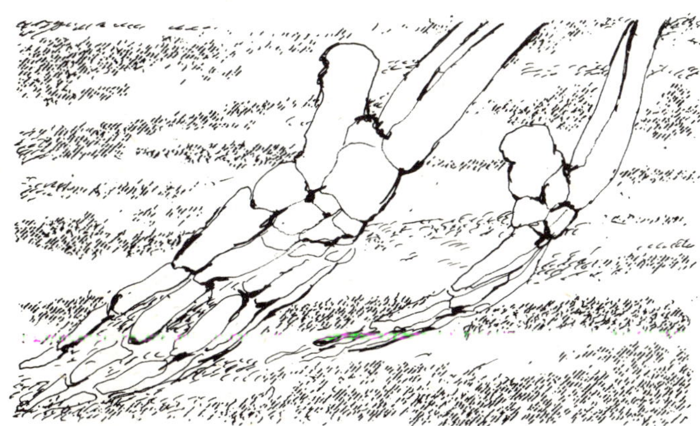

64 Whose pigs are these?

four-part round

Whose pigs are these?
Whose pigs are these?
They are John Potts', you can tell 'em by the spots,
And I found 'em in the vicarage garden.

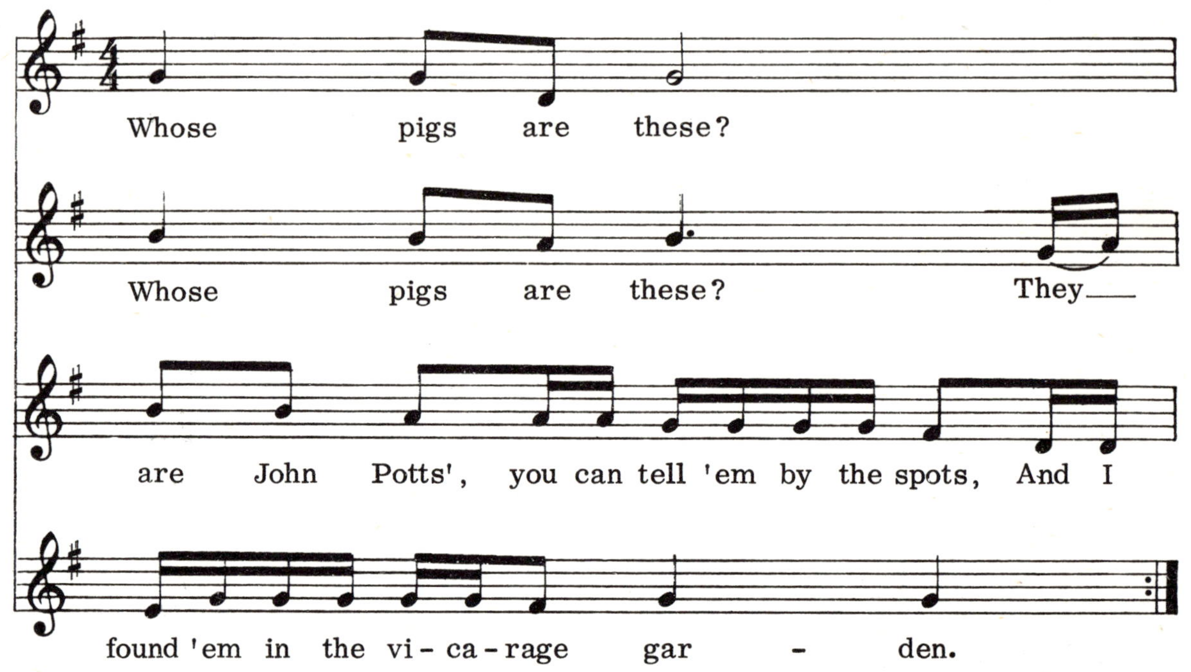

65 The barmaid from Swale

four-part round

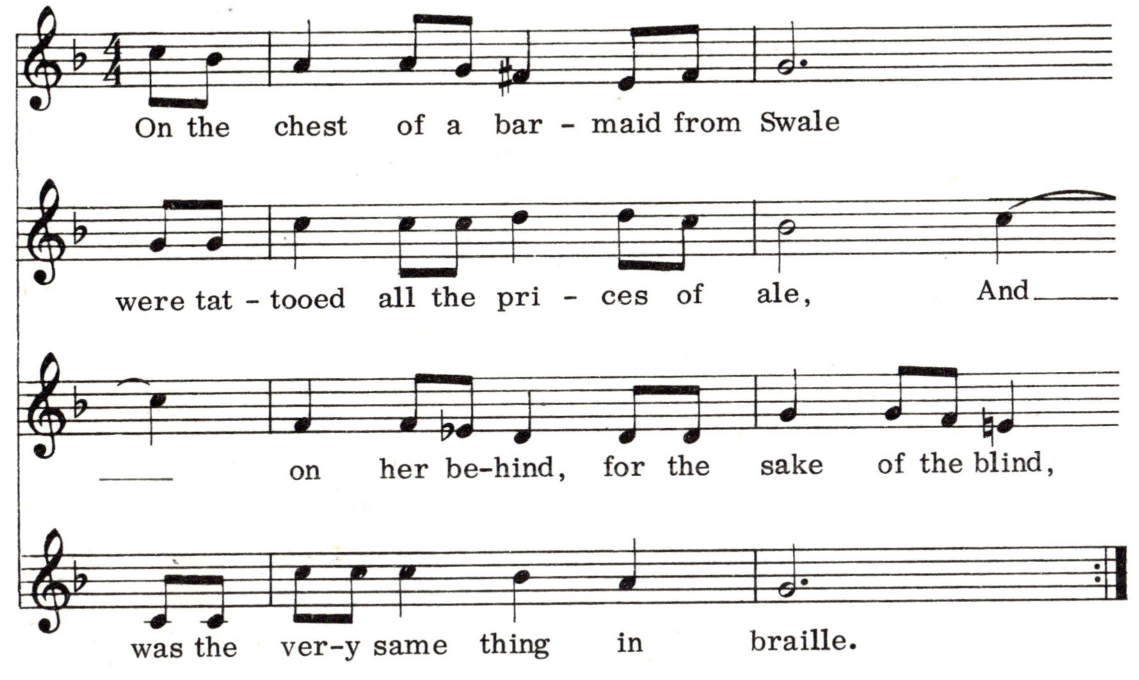

On the chest of a barmaid from Swale
Were tattooed all the prices of ale,
And on her behind,
For the sake of the blind,
Was the very same thing in braille.

66 Lady Madonna

1 Lady Madonna, children at your feet,
Wonder how you manage to make ends meet;
Who finds the money when you pay the rent?
Did you think that money was heaven sent?
Friday night arrives without a suitcase,
Sunday morning creeping like a nun,
Monday's child has learned to tie his bootlace,
See how they run.

2 Lady Madonna, baby at your breast,
Wonder how you manage to feed the rest.
Lady Madonna, lying on the bed,
Listen to the music playing in your head.
Tuesday afternoon is never-ending,
Wednesday morning papers didn't come,
Thursday night your stockings needed mending,
See how they run.

Lady Madonna, children at your feet,
Wonder how you manage to make ends meet.

GUITAR CHORDS
B7sus to B7 (bar 16) is an easy chord change:

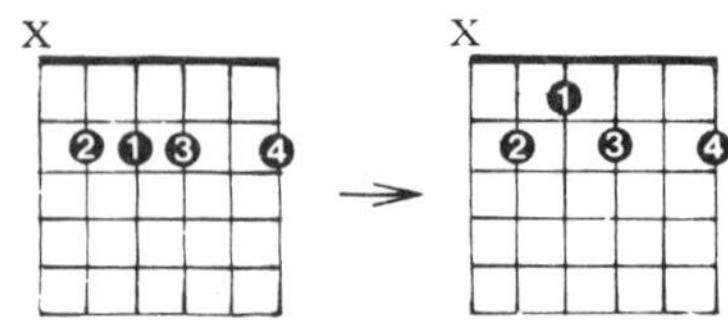

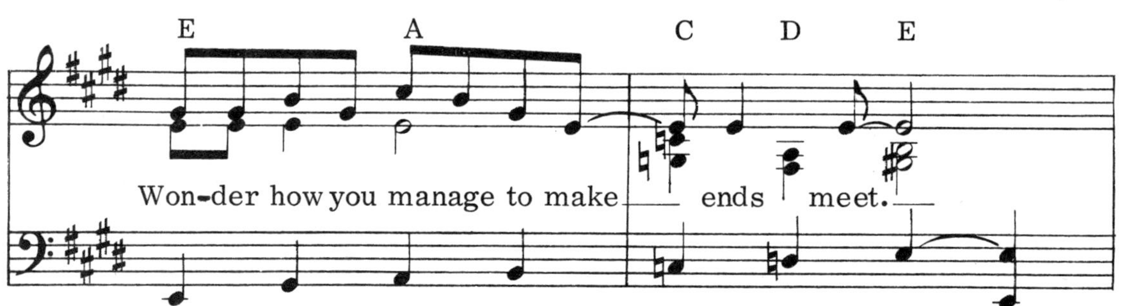

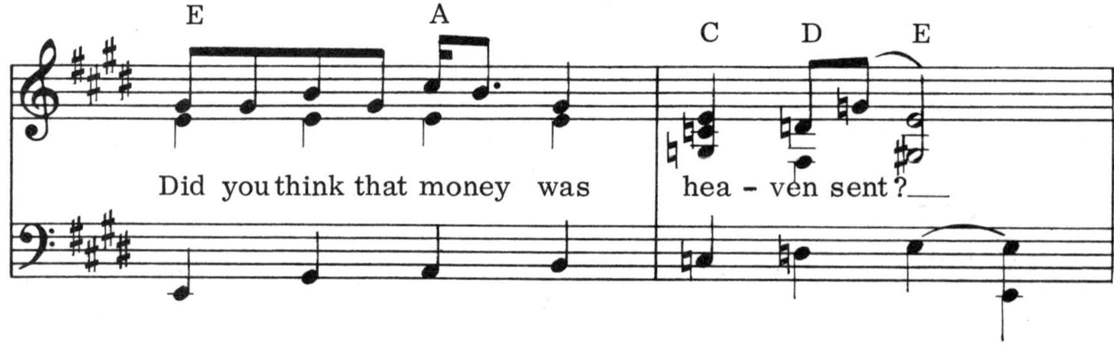

words and music: John Lennon and Paul MacCartney

67 Penny Lane

1 In Penny Lane there is a barber showing photographs
Of every head he's had the pleasure to know,
And all the people that come and go
Stop and say "hello".

2 On the corner is a banker with a motor car,
The little children laugh at him behind his back,
And the banker never wears a mac
In the pouring rain.
Very strange.

> Penny Lane is in my ears and in my eyes.
> There beneath the blue suburban skies I sit, and
> Meanwhile, back

3 In Penny Lane there is a fireman with an hour-glass,
And in his pocket is a portrait of the Queen.
He likes to keep his fire-engine clean,
It's a clean machine.

> Penny Lane is in my ears and in my eyes.
> A four of fish and finger pies in summer.
> Meanwhile, back

4 Behind the shelter in the middle of the roundabout
The pretty nurse is selling poppies from a tray.
And though she feels as if she's in a play,
She is anyway.

5 In Penny Lane the barber shaves another customer,
We see the banker sitting waiting for a trim,
And then the fireman rushes in
From the pouring rain.
Very strange.

> Penny Lane is in my ears and in my eyes.
> There beneath the blue suburban skies I sit, and
> Meanwhile back,
> Penny Lane is in my ears and in my eyes.
> There beneath the blue suburban skies,
> Penny Lane.

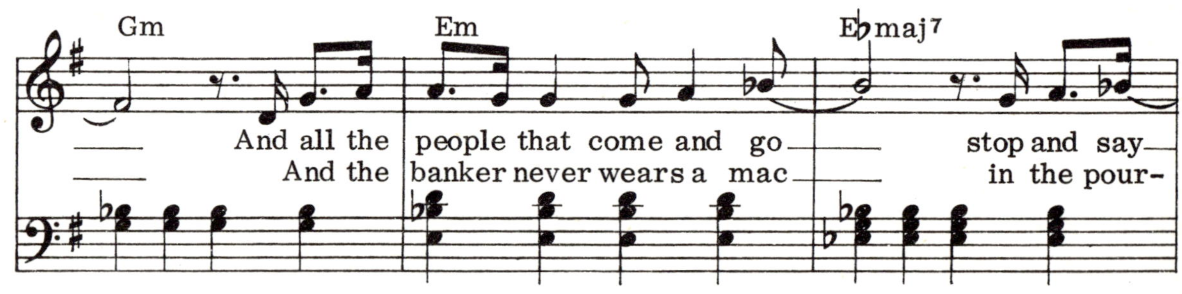

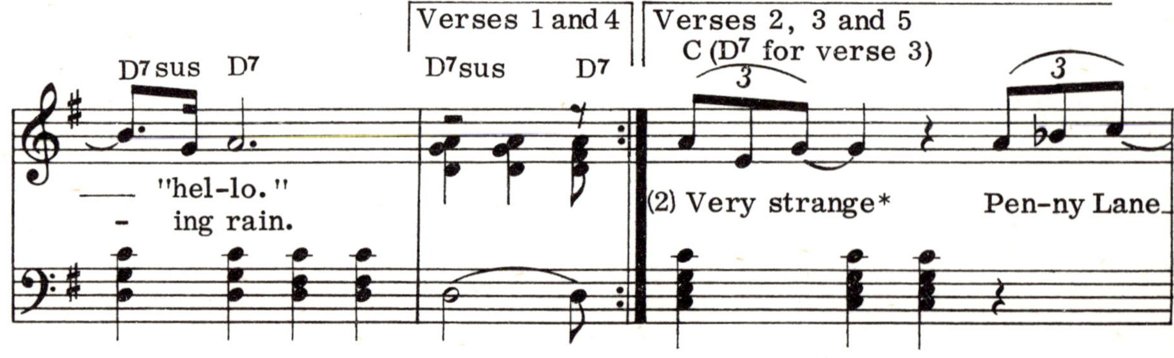

*In verse 3 the words "very strange" are left out, and accompanists play D7 instead of C.

E♭maj7

D7 sus

words and music: John Lennon and Paul MacCartney

68 The windmills of your mind

Round like a circle in a spiral,
  like a wheel within a wheel,
Never ending or beginning
  on an ever spinning reel,
Like a snowball down a mountain,
  or a carnival balloon,
Like a carousel that's turning
  running rings around the moon,
Like a clock whose hands are sweeping
  past the minutes of its face,
And the world is like an apple
  whirling silently in space,
Like the circles that you find
  in the windmills of your mind.

Like a tunnel that you follow
  to a tunnel of its own,
Down a hollow to a cavern
  where the sun has never shone,
Like a door that keeps revolving
  in a half-forgotten dream,
Or the ripples from a pebble
  someone tosses in a stream,
Like a clock whose hands are sweeping
  past the minutes of its face,
And the world is like an apple
  whirling silently in space,
Like the circles that you find
  in the windmills of your mind.

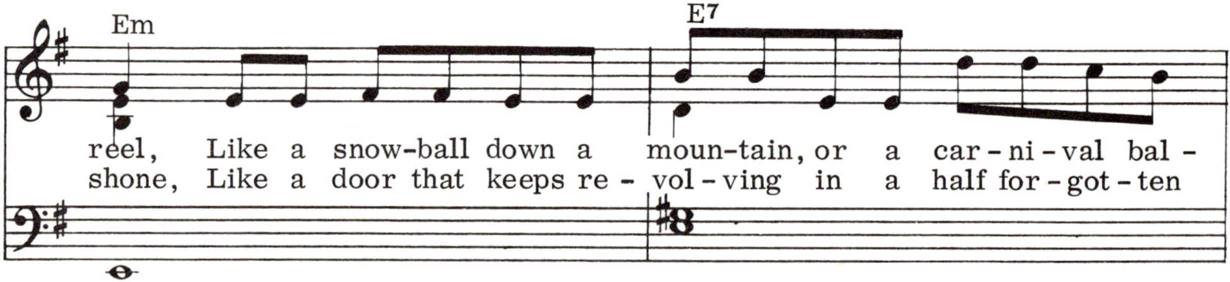

continued over . . .

Keys that jingle in your pocket,
  words that jangle in your head,
Why did summer go so quickly?
  Was it something that you said?
Lovers walk along a shore
  and leave their footprints in the sand,
Is the sound of distant drumming
  just the fingers of your hand?
Pictures hanging in a hallway
  and the fragment of a song,
Half-remembered names and faces,
  but to whom do they belong?
When you knew that it was over
  you were suddenly aware
That the autumn leaves were turning
  to the colour of her hair.

Like a circle in a spiral,
  like a wheel within a wheel,
Never ending or beginning
  on an ever spinning reel,
As the images unwind,
Like the circles that you find
In the windmills of your mind.

GUITAR CHORDS: Don't be put off by the unusual chords – they're not difficult:

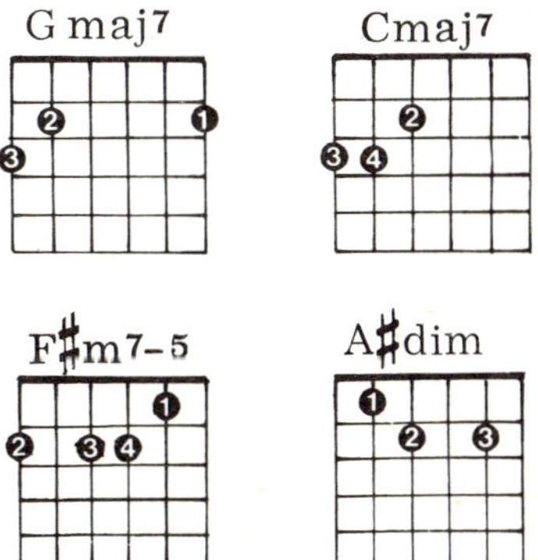

Am7
head, Why did sum-mer go so
D7
quick-ly? Was it some-thing that you
Gmaj7
said? Lo-vers walk a - long a
G7
shore and leave their foot-prints in the
Cmaj7
sand. Is the sound of dis-tant
F♯7
drum-ming just the fin-gers of your
Bm7
hand? Pic-tures hang-ing in a
E7
hall-way and the frag-ment of a
Am
song, Half re-membered names and
D7
fa-ces, but to whom do they be -
Gmaj7
long? When you knew that it was
Cmaj7
o - ver you were sud-den-ly a -

words: Marilyn and Alan Bergman
music: Michel Legrand

69 An Eriskay love lilt

traditional

Vair me oro van o,
Vair me oro van ee,
Vair me oru o ho,
Sad am I without thee.

1 When I'm lonely, dear white heart,
Black the night, or wild the sea,
By love's light my foot finds
The old pathway to thee.
Vair me oro van o . . .

2 Thou'rt the music of my heart,
Harp of joy, oh cruit mo chridh,
Moon of guidance by night,
Strength and light thou'rt to me.
Vair me oro van o . . .

cruit mo chridh: harp of my heart, pronounced "crootch mo chree".

70 Sailing

1 I am sailing, I am sailing,
Home again, 'cross the sea.
I am sailing stormy waters
To be near you, to be free.

2 I am flying, I am flying,
Like a bird, 'cross the sky.
I am flying, passing high clouds,
To be with you, to be free.

3 Can you hear me, can you hear me
Through the dark night far away?
I am dying, forever trying
To be with you, who can say?

4 We are sailing, we are sailing
Home again 'cross the sea.
We are sailing stormy waters
To be near you, to be free.

words and music: Gavin Sutherland

71 The yellow rose of Texas

1 There's a yellow rose in Texas
That I am going to see,
Nobody else can have her,
Nobody, only me.
She cried so when I left her,
It nearly broke my heart,
And if I ever find her
We never more will part.

She's the sweetest little rosebud
That Texas ever knew,
Her eyes are bright as diamonds,
They sparkle like the dew.
You can talk about your dearest
May
And sing of Rosa Lee,
But the yellow rose of Texas
Is the only girl for me.

2 Where the Rio Grande is flowing
And the starry skies are bright,
She walks along the river
In the quiet summer night;
She thinks, if I remember,
When we parted long ago,
I promised to come back again
And not to leave her so.

3 O now I'm going to find her,
For my heart is full of woe;
We'll sing the songs together
We sang so long ago;
We'll play the banjo gaily
And sing the songs of yore,
And the yellow rose of Texas
Will be mine for evermore.

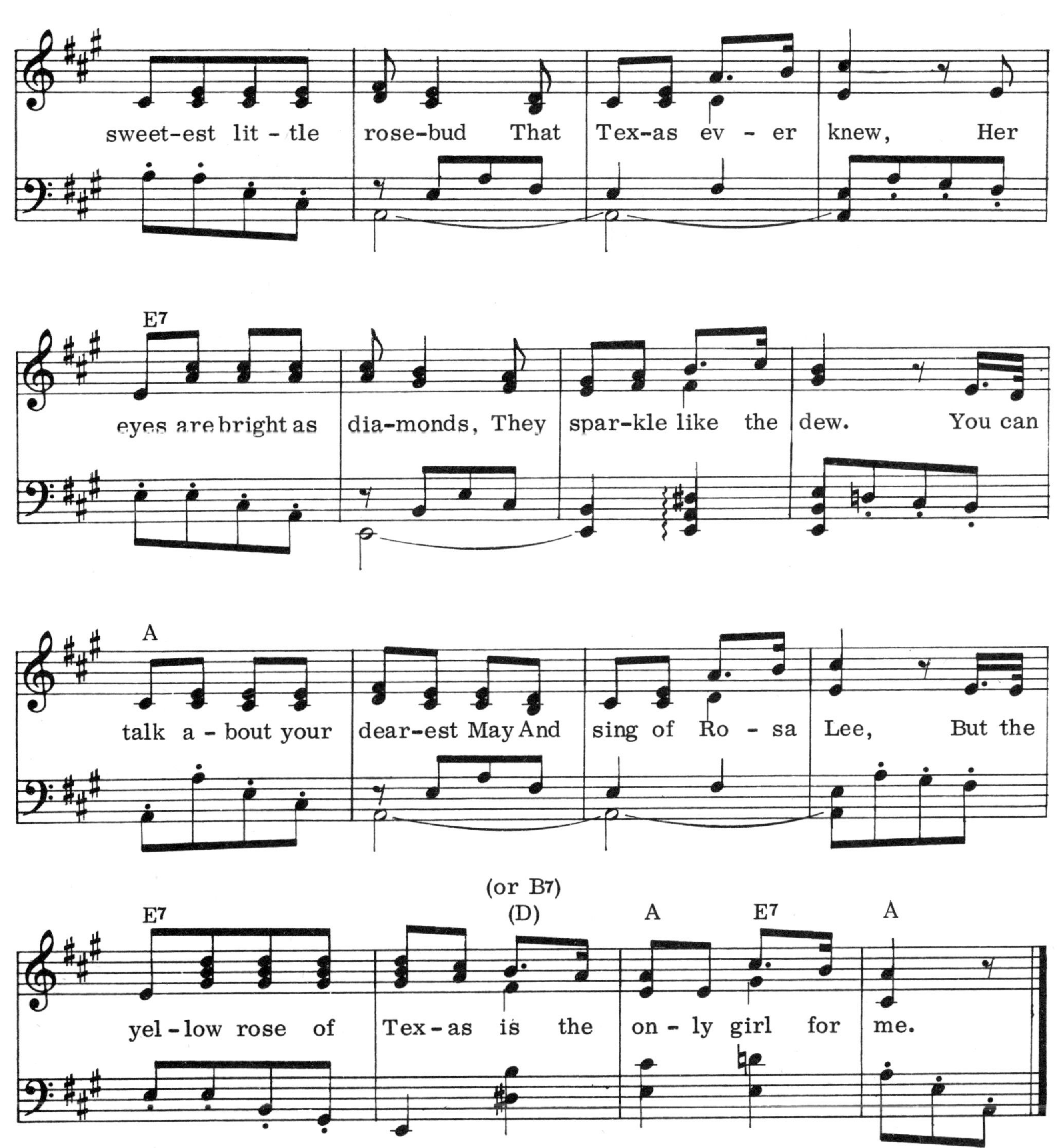
sweet-est lit - tle rose-bud That Tex-as ev - er knew, Her
E7
eyes are bright as dia-monds, They spar-kle like the dew. You can
A
talk a - bout your dear-est May And sing of Ro - sa Lee, But the
E7
(or B7)
(D)
A
E7
A
yel - low rose of Tex - as is the on - ly girl for me.

72 Messing about on the river

1 When the weather is fine then you know it's a sign
For messing about on the river.
If you take my advice, there's nothing so nice
As messing about on the river.
There are long boats and short boats and all sorts of craft,
And cruisers and keel boats and some with no draught.
So take off your coat and hop in a boat,
Go messing about on the river.

2 There are boats made from kits that reach you in bits,
For messing about on the river,
Or you might like to scull in a fibre-glass hull,
Just messing about on the river.
There are tillers and rudders and anchors and cleats,
And ropes that are sometimes referred to as sheets.
With the wind in your face, there's no finer place
Than messing about on the river.

3 There are skippers and mates, and rowing club eights,
Just messing about on the river.
There are pontoons and trots, and all sorts of knots,
For messing about on the river.
With inboards and outboards and dinghies you sail,
The first thing you learn is the right way to bail.
In a one-seat canoe you're skipper and crew,
Just messing about on the river.

D G C G D

-bout on the ri-ver. There are long boats and short boats and all sorts of

G C G A7 D G

craft, and cruis-ers and keel boats and some with no draught. So take off your

D C D G

coat and hop in a boat, Go mess-ing a - bout on the ri-ver.

words and music: Tony Hatch

4 There are bridges and locks and moorings and docks
When messing about on the river.
There's a whirlpool and weir that you mustn't go near
When messing about on the river.
  There are back-water places all hidden from view,
  And quaint little islands just waiting for you,
So I'll leave you right now to cast off your bow,
To go messing about on the river.

73 The lightning tree

words and music: Stephen Francis

74 I can see for miles

The song is presented here in its basic form, but The Who, in their recording of it, expand it slightly, doing a short instrumental break after verse 2 (using the harmonic scheme of the first five bars) and then returning to the beginning ("I know you've deceived me . . .") before leading into verse 3, which they sing in a higher key.

words and music: Peter Townshend

75 Scarborough Fair

1 Are you going to Scarborough Fair?
Parsley, sage, rosemary and thyme
Remember me to one who lives there,
She once was a true love of mine.

2 Tell her to make me a cambric shirt
Parsley, sage, rosemary and thyme
Without any seam or needlework,
Then she'll be a true love of mine.

traditional

3 Tell her to wash it in yonder dry well
Parsley, sage, rosemary and thyme
Where water ne'er sprung, nor drop of rain fell,
Then she'll be a true love of mine.

4 Tell her to dry it on yonder thorn
Parsley, sage, rosemary and thyme
Which never bore blossom since Adam was born,
Then she'll be a true love of mine.

5 Are you going to Scarborough Fair?
Parsley, sage, rosemary and thyme
Remember me to one who lives there,
She once was a true love of mine.

76 The wild mountain thyme

words and music: Francis McPeake

1 O the summer-time is coming,
And the trees are sweetly blooming,
And the wild mountain thyme
Grows around the blooming heather.

Will ye go, lassie, go,
And we'll all go together
To pull wild mountain thyme
All around the blooming heather,
Will ye go, lassie, go.

2 I will build my love a tower
Near yon pure crystal fountain,
And on it I will build
All the flowers of the mountain.
Will ye go, lassie, go . . .

3 If my true love she were gone
I would surely find another,
Where wild mountain thyme
Grows around the blooming heather.
Will ye go, lassie, go . . .

77 Thank U very much

continued over . . .

verse 5 (contd.)
(spoken)
D E D E D E D E D E D E
(5) cul-tur-al he-ri-tage, na-tion-al beverage, Be-ing fat, Un-i-on Jack, Nur-se-ry rhymes, Sun-day Times,
D E D E D E A
Thank U ve-ry much, thank U ve-ry ve-ry ve-ry ve-ry ve-ry ve-ry ve-ry ve-ry much.
Verse 6
D A D E D E
6. Thank U ve-ry much for buy-ing this song book, Thank U ve-ry much, thank U ve-ry ve-ry ve-ry much,
A D A D E A
Thank U ve-ry much for buying this song book, Thank U ve-ry ve-ry ve-ry much.
Verse 7
C Am Dm G F G F G
7. Thank U very much for our gra - cious team, Thank U ve-ry much, thank U ve-ry ve-ry ve-ry much,

words and music: Michael McGear

1 Thank u very much for the Aintree Iron,
Thank u very much, thank u very very very much,
Thank u very much for the Aintree Iron,
Thank u very very very much.

2 Thank u very much for the birds and bees,
Thank u very much, thank u very very very much,
Thank u very much for the birds and bees,
Thank u very very very much.

3 Thank u very much for the family circle,
Thank u very much, thank u very very very much,
Thank u very much for the family circle,
Thank u very very very much.

4 Thank u very much for . . (*spoken*) love,
Thank u very much, thank u very very very much,
Thank u very much for . . (*spoken*) love,
Thank u very very very much.

5 Thank u very much for the Sunday joint,
Thank u very much, thank u very very very much,
Thank u very much for the Sunday joint,
And our cultural heritage, national beverage,
Being fat, Union Jack,
Nursery rhymes, Sunday Times . . .
Thank u very much, thank u very very very very
very very very very much.

6 Thank u very much for buying this song book,
Thank u very much, thank u very very very much,
Thank u very much for buying this song book,
Thank u very very very much.

7 Thank u very much for our gracious team,
Thank u very much, thank u very very very much,
Thank u very much for our gracious team,
Thank u very much, thank u very very very very
very very very very . . (*spoken*) much.

Acknowledgements

The following copyright owners have kindly granted their permission for the reprinting of words and music:

ATV Music Ltd for 66 'Lady Madonna', © 1968 Northern Songs Ltd for the world, and 67 'Penny Lane', © 1967 Northern Songs Ltd for the world.

R. V. Beaumont for the music of 23 'Colonel Fazackerley'.

Boosey & Hawkes Music Publishers Ltd for 69 'An Eriskay love lilt', © 1909 Boosey & Co Ltd, reprinted from *Songs of the Hebrides* by permission of the Estate of M. Kennedy Fraser and Boosey & Hawkes Music Publishers Ltd.

Box & Cox Publications for 37 'The gypsy rover'.

Sydney Bron Music Co Ltd for 18 'Across the hills', 21 'My last cigarette' and 22 'I'm the urban spaceman'.

Judith Bush for 41 'Green lanes'.

Chappell Music Ltd for 8 'Settle-Carlisle railway', 11 'The broadside man' and 42 'Land of the old and grey', all © 1970 EFDS Publications Ltd, and for 14 'Bob the pedigree sheepdog', © 1974 EFDS Publications Ltd, and 76 'Wild mountain thyme', © 1962 EFDS Publications Ltd.

Chevron Music Publishing Ltd for 73 'The lightning tree'.

Crown Publishers Inc for 19 'Pollution', from *Tom Lehrer's Second Song Book*.

Ted Edwards for 9 'Coal-hole cavalry'.

EMI Music Publishing Ltd, 138-140 Charing Cross Road, London WC2H 0LD for 24 'Where did you get that hat?', © 1890 Francis Day & Hunter Ltd, 25 'The Field of the Willows', © 1969 Robbins Music Corp Ltd, and 43 'If it wasn't for the 'ouses in between', © 1894 Francis Day & Hunter Ltd.

Essex Music International Ltd for 7 'Indeed I would', 49 'The Marco Polo' and 56 'Sweet Willie', all © Harmony Music Ltd, and for 17 'Leave them a flower', © Durham Music Ltd, 60 'Liverpool Lou', © Coda Music Ltd, 74 'I can see for miles', © Fabulous Music Ltd, and the music of 12 'Timothy Winters'.

Folktracks and Soundpost Publications, The Centre for Oral Traditions, Grapevine House, Harberton, Totnes, Devon TQ9 7SE, for 39 'Dorset is beautiful'.

Noel Gay Music Co Ltd for 4 'Right said Fred', 5 'Hole in the ground' and 77 'Thank U very much', all © Noel Gay Music Co Ltd, and for 13 'Pete was a lonely mongrel dog', © Wednesday Music Ltd.

Heath Levy Music Co Ltd for 16 'Cotton Jenny'.

David Higham Associates Ltd for the words of 12 'Timothy Winters' and 23 'Colonel Fazackerley'.

John Hosier for the words of 61 'The orchestra song'.

Island Music Ltd for 70 'Sailing'.

Dick James Music Ltd, Chappell & Co (Australia) Pty Ltd, Dick James Music Inc (New York) and Leeds Music (Africa) Pty Ltd for 72 'Messing about on the river'.

Logo Songs Ltd for 3 'The gulls o' Invergordon', © Heathside Music Ltd/Logo Songs Ltd, and 26 'Mole in a hole', © 1974 Leading Note Ltd.

Maypole Music Ltd for 40 'Fling it here, fling it there'.

Mockbeggar Music, 24 Beresford Road, Wallasey, Merseyside L45 0JJ, for 38 'The Ellen Vannin tragedy', © Mockbeggar Music.

Simon & Schuster for 63 'Have you seen the ghost of Tom?', from *The Fireside Book of Children's Songs* by Marie Winn, © 1966 Marie Winn and Allan Miller, reprinted by permission of Simon & Schuster, a division of Gulf & Western Corporation.

United Artists Music Ltd for 20 'Air', from *Hair*, and 68 'The windmills of your mind'.

Voggenreiter Verlag (Bonn) for 61 'The orchestra song'.

World Around Songs (Burnsville, N.C. 28714) for 52 'Fulera mama', © 1958 World Around Songs Inc.

Index of titles and first lines

First lines are printed like this, *titles are printed like this.*